T0354657

One of the things I love most about the author of this book is her ability to see deep scriptural truths lived out in the day-to-day. This book takes personal moments from her daily life and draws correlations between our parenting and God's parenting—between our tendencies and God's tendencies, encouraging us to pray for change in our areas of weakness. I highly encourage young moms to take moments to slow down and reflect by going through Christine's study *Clean Home, Messy Heart*.

Beth Cortez, Pastor's Wife, Mother of 4

Clean Home, Messy Heart serves as a needed reminder that not a day of struggle or a moment of defeat goes by without the tending of our hearts by a loving Savior. It's a Scripture-filled encouragement to cling to God as He molds and shapes us through every facet of our lives.

Christina Nunez, Home Childcare Owner, Mother of 3

A lot of things about parenting are unique, but some things are universal. This book exposes the universal challenges that all parents face and reveals how God uses our children to open our eyes to our own hearts. It doesn't matter how young or old our children may be; the Lord parents us as we parent them. The pages in *Clean Home, Messy Heart* give us his words, which address our hearts and empower us to persevere in our mission to "train up our children." Listen up and be encouraged while you read this book. Laugh, cry, and praise God that he understands everything there is to know about parenting.

Kelly Merlo, Grandmother of 5, Mother of 3

As you read this book, it's clear that Christine has spent time with Jesus, learning about his wisdom and truth for women and moms. I love how she opens up her life, showing us what God is teaching her through her little ones. She is sincere, raw, and humble; each of those things help to soften our hearts to be taught alongside her. This is not a one-time read—it's a devotional, full of Scripture references to help us take an even closer look at ourselves. This is a book I will be pouring over again and again.

Stephanie Roberts, Pastor's Wife, Mother of 1

Clean Home, Messy Heart is an honest, real-life story of messiness covered by God's grace and mercy through the application of Scripture and prayer. Christine shares her experiences and raw feelings as a wife and mother, navigating life's daily challenges and blessings as she looks to God and his promises. She encourages others to focus on the Lord through his Word and provides excellent guidance for growth by way of prayer, memory verses, and study reflections suitable for individuals or small groups. I could read this book again and again and benefit from it each time.

Dana Rhoades, Teacher and ASL Community Interpreter, Mother of 2

As a homeschooling mom with four kids under the age of 9, I found this book to be a breath of fresh air. Christine understands how it feels to be a mom who falls short of her own expectations yet remembers to fall back on God's grace to handle what comes each day. This book is a must read for any woman who is struggling with motherhood and wants to find her peace in the only One who can give it: Jesus.

Jamie Fluken, Homeschool Teacher, Mother of 4

Clean Home, Messy Heart

Promises of Renewal, Hope, and Change for Overwhelmed Moms

Christine M. Chappell

WESTBOW
PRESS®
A DIVISION OF THOMAS NELSON
& ZONDERVAN

WestBow Press books may be ordered through booksellers or by contacting:

WestBow Press
A Division of Thomas Nelson & Zondervan
1663 Liberty Drive
Bloomington, IN 47403
www.westbowpress.com
1 (866) 928-1240

Because of the dynamic nature of the Internet, any web addresses or links contained in this book may have changed since publication and may no longer be valid. The views expressed in this work are solely those of the author and do not necessarily reflect the views of the publisher, and the publisher hereby disclaims any responsibility for them.

Any people depicted in stock imagery provided by Thinkstock are models, and such images are being used for illustrative purposes only.
Certain stock imagery © Thinkstock.

This book is a work of non-fiction. Unless otherwise noted, the author and the publisher make no explicit guarantees as to the accuracy of the information contained in this book and in some cases, names of people and places have been altered to protect their privacy.

Scripture quotations are from The Holy Bible, English Standard Version® (ESV®), copyright © 2001 by Crossway, a publishing ministry of Good News Publishers. Used by permission. All rights reserved.

Scripture taken from the Holy Bible, NEW INTERNATIONAL VERSION®. Copyright © 1973, 1978, 1984 by Biblica, Inc. All rights reserved worldwide. Used by permission. NEW INTERNATIONAL VERSION® and NIV® are registered trademarks of Biblica, Inc. Use of either trademark for the offering of goods or services requires the prior written consent of Biblica US, Inc.

Scripture quotations taken from the Holy Bible, New Living Translation, Copyright © 1996, 2004. Used by permission of Tyndale House Publishers, Inc., Wheaton, Illinois 60189. All rights reserved.

ISBN: 978-1-5127-3854-4 (sc)
ISBN: 978-1-5127-3855-1 (hc)
ISBN: 978-1-5127-3853-7 (e)

Library of Congress Control Number: 2016906408

Print information available on the last page.

WestBow Press rev. date: 04/25/2016

To my Dad, Timothy F. Strombel

God has not promised skies always blue,
Flower-strewn pathways all our lives through;
God has not promised sun without rain,
Joy without sorrow, peace without pain.

God has not promised we shall not know
Toil and temptation, trouble and woe;
He has not told us we shall not bear
Many a burden, many a care.

But God has promised strength for the day,
Rest for the labor, light for the way,
Grace for the trials, help from above,
Unfailing kindness, undying love.

Annie Johnson Flint (1886–1932),
"What God Has Promised"

Contents

Acknowledgements

Writing this book has been one of the most amazing journeys. Through it, I have experienced the presence of God in ways I never could have imagined. Truly he was the driving force behind these words, motivating me to keep pressing forward, despite my own peculiar fears of inadequacy. I do not hesitate to confess that without the power of the Holy Spirit pulling me through from start to finish and the dedicated prayers of many friends, you would never be holding this completed work in your hands. I thank the Lord for bringing Paul's words to life for me as I wrote this book: "Not that we are sufficient in ourselves to claim anything as coming from us, but our sufficiency is from God." (2 Corinthians 3:5)

Thank you to my husband, Brett, for making me a mother to three beautiful children. Thank you for your words of encouragement, your faithful love, and for supporting the calling of the Lord in my life. Thank you for every step we have taken together on our journey thus far, even the steps that started on shifting sands. Praise God, we now have a solid rock on which to build a foundation together, hand-in-hand, reaching out towards eternity.

Thank you to my mother, Diane Sarazen, for the years of love, heartaches, sacrifices, and tears you have endured to give me the best start in the world as humanly possible. It does not go unnoticed how your heart has bled for your children in indescribable ways. Thank you for giving us an example of what it means to live and love regardless of circumstances. Most of all, thank you for loving my Father at his best and also at his weakest, 'til death separated him from your arms. I smile to think of what the Lord has in store for your journey ahead. I love you always.

My precious babies, Brianna, Cash and Charlotte—I am so grateful to be your mother and to grow together in our knowledge of the Lord. I am thankful that you give me grace to fail and love to forgive my mistakes. You all are such an important part of my life, and I am so blessed God has given you to your Father and me to care for, train up, and release into a world that needs your caring hearts. I promise I will continue to grow in my ability to love you the way God loves us, thanks to the boundless love of Christ.

Thank you to my manuscript advisors Barbra Burgess, Kelly Merlo, and Nancy Albao, who have spent hours reading, advising, editing, praying, and counseling me before, during and after this manuscript development. Most of all, thank you for loving me through all of my bouts with doubt and fear. I would not know the importance of *being a disciple* of Christ if God had not brought Barbra into my life. I would not have learned to *walk as a disciple* of Christ if God had not brought Kelly into my life. And I would not have seen what it means to *persevere as a disciple* of Christ if God had not brought Nancy into my life. Truly, I am grateful beyond measure for these women, for they have fully embraced the Titus 2 command and made it their life's passion to train up the next generation of sisters in Christ.

I am so appreciative of the efforts of my manuscript editor Chelsey Harlan, who generously provided the value of clarity as she combed through these pages to see errors I could not. Her enthusiasm for the content was tremendously uplifting; a sorely needed boost toward the end of the long publishing process.

Thank you to the leadership of my church, Covenant Grace. Not long ago, I was an outsider attending church with extreme discomfort—mere weeks after my father had passed away from cancer. The encouragement and love I have been given from Pastor Sabo Cortez and many others has not ceased to this day; I simply would not be a student of the Word if it weren't for the teaching and equipping I have received through my church body. Many thanks to Pastor Sabo and Pastor Erick Cobb for their guidance, support, and mentorship—necessities for an enthusiastic new believer striving to put off the old self and put on the new (Ephesians 4:20–24).

Lastly, thank you to the special ladies of my discipleship group: Colleen Buck, Dana Rhoades, Melissa Orr, and Sherina Lee. Under Kelly's direction and leading, we have all grown leaps and bounds in our desire to crave God's Word on a daily basis. I am thankful for the hundreds of prayers these friends have prayed over me and this book, and am honored to watch God work in marvelous ways in their own hearts. These truly are precious moments together—only a foretaste of what's to come.

And let the peace of Christ rule in your hearts, to which indeed you were called in one body. And be thankful. Let the word of Christ dwell in you richly, teaching and admonishing one another

in all wisdom, singing psalms and hymns and spiritual songs, with thankfulness in your hearts to God. And whatever you do, in word or deed, do everything in the name of the Lord Jesus, giving thanks to God the Father through him. Colossians 3:15–17 ESV

Forward

Some writers come to the table with the goal of changing lives, and everything they write is filtered through the lens of "Will this change the world?" And then, some writers have a fire of a message burning inside their hearts, urging a way out—it comes in the form of letters, sentences, and stories of imperfection, beautifully laced together. The end goal: for one woman to be able to read it and silently sigh, "Me too."

Christine's book, *Clean Home, Messy Heart,* is, without a doubt, the latter. It's identifiable, as each story will have you either giggling or crying because *you just know.* You can see your own crayon-stained walls and pen-etched coffee tables; you can recall those drives home from school where you wanted to be paying attention but completely zoned out on your baby's recount of her day.

Its pages are filled with rich Scripture, dissected and applied to our everyday situations of womanhood. The busyness gets all of us—and if we're being totally and completely honest, our ugly comes out on our kids and husbands more than we'd like to admit. Sometimes, the Morlet home puts reality TV to shame. *Can I get an "Amen?"*

It would be easy to read through the questions and prayers at the end of each chapter as a bystander, but please hear me when I say the experience of these pages will be so much richer with your active participation. Answer the questions—in a journal (Marshall's and Ross are my personal journal black hole #yourewelcome). Down the road, you will cherish seeing the journey this book takes you through.

Memorize the Scriptures. Sing them, meditate on them, write them on index cards and scatter them around your house. Let your kids color them or make it a family activity. Hiding God's Word in the depths of your heart might not feel like a major investment now, but one day you will pull it out of nowhere when you least expect, and will be so grateful for it.

Lastly, pray the prayers...all day long. Customize them for your own heart, your own family, your own marriage and friendships and parenting. They're so honest—and God, *he ain't got time for the frill!* He just wants our open, raw, undressed-up thoughts, emotions, and struggles. As I head into my own hidden season of motherhood, with a toddler and newborn in my circle, I am grateful for Christine's wisdom and vulnerability, which you will no doubt experience in these pages. I'm grateful that in the midst of my crazy, I can read her journey and sigh, "Girl, me too."

Julianna Morlet, Worship Leader at Shoreline Church in Austin, Texas

Learn more about Julianna by visiting her blog at juliannamorlet.com, finding her on Facebook at facebook.com/juliannamorlet, or on Twitter/Instagram @juliannamorlet

Introduction

The baby was screaming, the eldest was arguing, and the toddler was pleading for milk while my husband lay crippled on the couch with a headache. It was the sort of unwelcome symphony that puts a mother's guts into a knot while blending her wearied mind to a chunky soup.

In moments like these, when the swirling thoughts in my mind can be classified a category 5 hurricane, it's hard not to jump completely out of my skin with a roar of anger. On other occasions, I'm trapped in the throes of depression and numbing indifference. Though everything and everyone around me seems to move at one hundred miles an hour, I can only observe and react in wearied apathy.

Wrestling with my thoughts, emotions, and hectic home environment feels like a losing battle, most days. My desperate attempt to control my surroundings manifests itself in my fight to keep my home in a constant state of cleanliness. I dust tables, scrub floors, vacuum car seats and labor away at tidying up with every opportunity. I shriek when the milk has been strewn across the table and begrudgingly peel sticky popsicle sticks off the stained carpet.

My grass is never green enough, the flowers never well-watered, and the pet hair tumbleweeds continue to float across the floor no matter how many times I've swept. Yet, in spite of all of my efforts to control the cleanliness and order of our home, I'm left frustrated, joyless and defeated. This obsession with a well-manicured home serves to reflect my utter inability to clean my messy heart, worn from the stains of pride and bitterness, yet hanging by the thread of the gospel.

How can faith in Christ redeem my overwhelmed heart in the moments of everyday motherhood? I know Jesus is the *way* to the Father, the author of *truth,* and the source of abundant *life,* but how does this knowledge transform my heart in the middle of the temper tantrums and disobedience of my children? Can the good news of the gospel hold me together when I'm sorely split at the seams?

WHAT THIS BOOK ISN'T...AND WHAT IT IS

If you're looking for a book that offers self-help tips, this isn't the one for you. I am not going to divulge things you can be doing differently to win a prize for mother-of-the-year. I am also not going to give you a magical cure-all for your parenting woes. The answer to this dilemma does not lie in improved child behavior, an increased landscaping budget, or the ability to hire a weekly maid service. The solution to feeling overwhelmed is not *something,* but rather *someone*: Jesus Christ.

Do you know him? I don't mean know *about* him; I mean know who he was, who he is, and who he promises to be to us in the future? If you do not have a personal relationship with Christ but are curious about him and the good news of his life, death, and resurrection, please visit the resource section at the back of this book. These chapters cannot stand apart from the foundation of Christ, our Savior.

Now, if you're looking for a fellow sister in Christ to share honest experiences of God's grace in the midst of anxiety-riddled highs or melancholy lows, you've found a friend who knows your burden. I'm not writing as one who has been there, but I am sharing as someone *who is there*, determined to keep focused on the rescuing grace God supplies by way of the cross. It's a grace that is always available to us in our time of need; a transforming grace that promises not to leave us where we lie, even when we cannot bear to lift another dirty dish or soiled diaper.

THE JOURNEY AHEAD TOGETHER

Warning: these pages contain real-life spiritual breakdowns. While it isn't easy to air my dirty laundry, the pill is easier to swallow when it brings God all the glory. Why on earth he decides to step down into my messy life is something I've yet to fully understand. Regardless, I will forever be grateful he doesn't remain so high and lofty that I cannot reach him in my most desperate moments. He bends a knee and lends an ear with but a whimper from my lips.

Each chapter recounts an actual story of various interactions with my three little darlings—the very creatures God uses to reveal my messy heart struggles. We'll take a deeper look at various convictions the Holy Spirit has brought to mind during these incidents, and then soak ourselves in the Word of God for therapeutic relief. We'll linger much longer (as we should) on the soothing balm that is *the Word of the Lord*. Though these are my stories, they're also small glimpses into common heart ailments many of us face, certainly as women but especially as mothers.

Though I highlight three main Scriptures per story, you'll find I've also alluded to supplemental verses in the text. I encourage you to look up and explore these additional Scriptures on your own—don't just skim by them as flabby excess to toss aside. Make a commitment to yourself to use a journal along with this book to chronicle your own discoveries as you use God's Word to help transform your own heart. You may also consider taking a look at the *Clean Home, Messy Heart Reflection Journal* to accompany your travels through these chapters. You can learn more about this journal by visiting www.faithfulsparrow.com/CHMHjournal.

There is no substitute for time spent reading an open Bible. Whatever nuggets of wisdom you may glean from the words in this book pale in comparison to the Spirit-illumined revelations you'll receive spending time in the living Word. While many of us have developed techniques and habits for enriching our time spent reading the Bible, I'm happy to share some things that have worked well for me. Should you be interested in jump-starting your study time with some simple tips, visit the resource section at the conclusion of this book.

There's one feature particularly special to me (that I hope is a blessing to you)—the closing prayers at the conclusion of each chapter. These are special because both you and I need to believe we're not alone in the sorrows and anxieties that motherhood can conjure up. I have not earned a motherhood or discipleship doctorate that makes me immune to the pitfalls of depressive moods or intense worries. These prayers are inclusive of *all* readers of this book who struggle to cling to the cross of Christ when hope for change seems lost. By praying these together during our pilgrimage through this book, we pray not only for ourselves but also for each other. Together, we bring our burdensome loads to the feet of the Father—exactly where they belong.

Lastly, each section provides questions designed to help store up the Word of God into our hearts through study reflection, memorization, and prayer. The amount of blessing and growth you receive from this book will be directly correlated to the amount of time you allow God's Word to cut to your core. This book has the option of being used for individual study or as a small group curriculum. Whichever you may choose, be blessed by allowing God to speak to you through faithfully journaling your responses at the conclusion of each section.

Being open and honest with ourselves is often difficult. I'm hopeful this collection of stories will help alleviate any fears of being humbly transparent with yourself, compelling you to turn your mess over to the heavenly hands that will make something beautiful from it. Rest assured, God will pour out his grace upon the time you spend reflecting on this book and abiding in his Word, fulfilling his promise to bear good fruit in you as a result.

Dear sisters, let us approach the throne of grace to find our refreshing reprieve. Let's praise the Lord as we find encouragements in Scripture which console our aching and weary souls. May we be filled with a peace that surpasses all understanding as we huddle under the cross together, adjoined by the Spirit through faith and accepted by the Father through grace.

**We're surrounded by the circumstances
he has ordained for our sanctification.**

When our perspective of this life is nearsighted, we
come to believe that what is in front of us is all there
is. We resist doing the awkward things entailed in
walking in love. We despise the hard work it takes
to run the race. We avoid the pain that results from
fighting for our faith by choosing not to fight at all.[1]

Gloria Furman

1

This Isn't Trouble

I had to walk outside to get away from it—the tension of my anger paired with the stubbornness of his tantrum. My toddler son decided I was encroaching upon his individual rights by simply trying to put on his T-shirt. As I wrestled with him to get the shirt on, he shrieked his objections, making it very clear such a mistreatment would not leave my ear drums unpunished.

"Oh, Lord!" I sighed, rolling my eyes to the ceiling in hopeless futility. Finally after several minutes of wrestling, repositioning, and grabbing various flailing limbs, I gave up. I summoned my husband to come deal with the meltdown, and then stormed out of the room in a desperate attempt to calm down—or more honestly, to cry.

Angst-ridden and defeated, I made my way to the crisp morning air of the backyard, coming to a stop at the fence. Unable to constrain my frustrated tears, I lowered my head into my hands, leaned against the wooden planks, and let my eyes flood with overwhelming emotion. I sniveled and sobbed like a toddler, all alone in my bubble of pity.

After the initial wave of tears had passed, I thumbed through my mental rolodex for just the right scripture to preach my heart off the ledge. I recalled the verse I had read the night prior: *God is our refuge and strength, a very present help in trouble* (Psalm 46:1). With that promise in mind, I began to pray, but I didn't get the comfort I was looking for.

THE MESSINESS OF LOVE

It wasn't long before my eyes were opened to the struggle going on inside of my heart. This situation certainly wasn't the "trouble" my prayer had made it out to be. After the Spirit had lifted the fog of frustration from my mind, I came to understand something else entirely: this wasn't trouble in the slightest, this was what love *required*. His gentle conviction about my complaint caused me to wonder how many times I had asked for relief from trouble, when all I wanted was relief from inconvenience. I thought about how quickly I was inclined to pray *Lord, deliver me from this problem* when I really meant *Lord, I don't want to love the way you ask me to*.

Red-eyed and humbled, I came to the regrettable conclusion that so often my pleas for rescue are uttered as requests to let my will be done. Whenever I feel my pride pinned to the ground, I wrestle a free arm to tap myself out. The minute God asks me to love the unlovable, I cry "Foul!" like the sorest of losers.

Though I was upset about the rebellion of my son, I recognized my inclination to conduct rebellions of my own. I don't usually get uncontested compliance from him, nor does God from me, especially when I'm asked to treat others how they *aren't* treating me. Feeling the Spirit's conviction led me to consider what real trouble looks like and, more importantly, what it doesn't. Sometimes deliverance from a predicament has more to do with the war *inside* our hearts than it does the battles we wage on the outside, be it on the frontlines or the changing tables.

WASHING WITH THE WORD

The gift of faith in Christ is not a promise of painlessness, but a promise of perseverance and transformation (James 1:3, Romans 5:3–4). As we seek Jesus for humility during our own rebellious flare-ups, we must ask ourselves one simple question: "Am I upset because I'm genuinely in trouble, or am I bitter because I'm being asked to *genuinely love?*" If our responses are typically the latter, then turning to God's Word can show us the way to love even in the most trying of times (2 Corinthians 7:10).

But God shows his love for us in that while we were still sinners, Christ died for us. Romans 5:8 ESV

Our Father knows all about loving the ugly. God sees the frailty of his fallen creation and knows the weakness of human flesh. He knows our frame (Psalm 103:14) and recognizes that we are trapped in the shambles of sin unless his righteous right hand pulls us out from the wreckage.

Thankfully, God long ago devised a plan to restore humanity back to the "very good" he had created in the beginning (Genesis 1:31)—he would send his Son into the mess. Jesus willingly volunteered to live the life of righteousness *we could not live* and to die the death *we should have died* so that we could stand justified[2] before the Father, welcomed and adored (2 Corinthians 5:21).

Our Father took on the roles of judge, jury, executioner, *and offender*. We easily forget the pain inflicted by such a plan of salvation. For the very first time in eternity, God the Father completely turned his face away from his only begotten Son. We need not go far to be reminded of the unimaginable despair this caused. Christ, bloodied and pierced, echoed the cry of Psalm 22:1 as he hung suffocating on the cross: "My God, my God, why have you forsaken me?" (Mark 15:34)

Our Lord endured excruciating rejection and punishment to earn our redemption. Jesus experienced complete separation from the Father so that we would never have to. God chose *love*—the sort of love that demonstrates the true meaning of "sacrificial". Our mocking, spitting, and push-back did nothing to change his mind or thwart the plan. As we were busy being blissfully caught up in our unrighteousness, God sent Christ. When we begin to deeply grasp this sort of faithful love, even the messiest heart can't help but sing:

> *How deep the Father's love for us, how vast beyond all measure*
> *That he should give his only Son, to make a wretch his treasure.*[3]

This is how we know what love is: Jesus Christ laid down his life for us. And we ought to lay down our lives for our brothers and sisters. 1 John 3:16 NIV

Christ *laid down* his life for us. An act of laying something down means you must first have possession and control over it. Jesus affirmed his authority to give his life as an acceptable sacrifice in our place (John 10:18). At no time was Jesus taken against his will, nor did he refuse the false accusations hurled against him. He very well knew the hearts of people and how they would reject him; nevertheless, he came (John 2:24–25). He is truly the Good Shepherd who laid his life down for his sheep (John 10:11). His submission to the plan of salvation was motivated by love and the joy that was set before him (Hebrews 12:2).

Jesus' voluntary sacrifice is the foundation on which biblical love for our family must be built. His example shows us how to love others, not because they deserve it, but because it's what God commands (Matthew 22:37–39). In order to pour his love out to us, he had to take up his cross and deny himself. It is into this mold we are shaped as we learn to love others through the laying down of *ourselves* (Luke 9:23). What makes Jesus' sacrifice even more amazing is the weight of the suffering he endured so he could utter, "It is finished" (John 19:30). The journey to Golgotha[4] proves the great lengths Jesus chose to travel for the sake of love—a love for the Father and a love for his people.

This kind of love softens our hearts when they harden from pride. Though it seems impossible to love the way he does (even just half of the time), the Spirit empowers us to press on towards the goal of being conformed to Christ's image

(Philippians 3:14). Because Christ chose to give us his life, Scripture encourages us to give ours to others—including children who behave in the most unlovable manner. To love sacrificially means to love without *prerequisite* or *requirement*. It means our love transcends behaviors, attitudes, and hurt. To love others as Christ loved us means we must be willing to lay aside our ego and bitterness for the joy set *before us*: a future crown of righteousness and of life (2 Timothy 4:8, James 1:12).

> *For the Spirit God gave us does not make us timid,*
> *but gives us power, love and self-discipline.*
> 2 Timothy 1:7 NIV

Though wrestling with my son over a T-shirt showed formidable strength, frustration overtook my heart, weakened by pride. I relied upon fleshly power to control the situation, yet was only able to display spiritual timidity by succumbing to anger. This is certainly not how to live by the power of the Spirit God has given us, but it takes time and experience to learn how to walk in a different manner than before (Galatians 5:16–17).

Power, love, and self-discipline—these are not things given so that we can exercise authority over others. These things are gifted to us so we can obey God's commandments. By the power of God, we have the ability to boldly love others when they don't deserve it (1 Thessalonians 3:12). By the love of Christ, we have an example of how to set aside our pride to repay evil with good (1 Peter 3:9). And by the self-discipline of the Holy Spirit, we have the wisdom to beat back our anger by setting our minds on things above, which promises life and peace (Colossians 3:2, Romans 8:5–6).

As the Spirit works through us to share God's love with others, he also works in us to make true sacrificial love the beat of our hearts. The gospel is what propels us forward when we feel completely spent. By faith and grace, our ability to love the way God loved us (John 3:16) begins to bear the luscious fruit of the Spirit (Galatians 5:22).

When things get supremely difficult, the Holy Spirit gives us the capability to walk through these transformative regenerations and the discipline to persevere. By grace and grace alone, we'll find a way to love in the fit and the fight. Though we're sure to have hiccups when it comes to loving well, in Christ we find the strength to keep trying.

BATHING IN PRAYER

Father, I thank you for the gracious love you poured out for me on the cross. I cannot begin to comprehend the pain and the grief it cost to love your creation in such a magnificent way. Lord, in my most desperate moments, you never fail to whisper reminders of your love and truth into my ears. I confess I often pray for changes in circumstances, but the real change I need is in my heart. Please grant me unwavering trust—that as I rely on your Word and your Spirit for change, you can and you will make it happen. I know it won't be instant, Father, but I do know that change will come. I ask for your mercies to rain down upon me as I rely on your grace to love others the way that you ask. Praise your name and your holy Son, amen.

HANGING HEARTS OUT TO DRY
STUDY REFLECTION:

Read John 3:16, Matthew 5:43–48, and Luke 6:27–36. In your own words, summarize what it looks like to love someone biblically.

MEMORIZATION:

For the Spirit God gave us does not make us timid, but gives us power, love and self-discipline.
2 Timothy 1:7 NIV

PRAYER:

Read Romans 5:8. This verse confirms that God loved us at our most unlovable state. Take a moment to write a prayer of gratitude and thanksgiving to the Lord for his steadfast love towards you, confess convictions that were brought to mind as you read this chapter, and ask for help to transform accordingly.

**Our sin is only bad news if we
don't have a Savior.**

Our slavery to sin has been broken. That doesn't
mean that we will never struggle against sin again
or that the struggle won't be desperate at times. But
it does mean that sin's power to condemn us, to fill
us with obedience-depleting guilt, is over.[1]
Elyse Fitzpatrick

2

Sin on the Table

There it was, carved ever so carefully into the wood: "B.C. + C.C." enclosed by a dainty heart. The romantic etching of our eldest daughter (who was 7 years old at the time) would have been darling on the tree in the backyard, but instead she chose the only spot on the family dining table that had gone unmarked by paint, scuff, or some other method of furniture destruction only a child could conjure up. While I appreciated the bold proclamation of love between her father and me, by no means was defacing property the way to go about expressing it.

Imagine my disbelief when, two years later, fresh new engravings peeked out from under the bowl of her morning cereal. Appearing as frustrated scribbles, these new markings completely overlaid the former, more carefully applied outlines.

The discovery left me speechless, not to mention astonished by her lack of good judgment.

At her first chance, she blamed the gouges on her two-year-old brother. However, my maternal detective skills knew the marks were far too deliberate for a toddler's abilities. I looked her straight in the eye and demanded she tell me whether or not she did it. Almost instantly, I saw the war in her heart. She was weighing the guilt of confession with the temptation to cover her tracks.

THE MESSINESS OF SIN

I leaned into her wide-eyed glaring silence, accepting her lack of defense as a submission to conviction. After a few harsh words about how she should know better, I threw my hands into the air and moved to break up the quarrelling babies in the other room. I juggled diapers, wipes, and legs while trying to figure out why on earth she would do this again. Why would she choose to do wrong, having previously been disciplined for the exact same behavior?

After giving it some thought, I realized I had mistakenly made the assumption that our daughter had *grown up* and subsequently *grown out* of being tempted to engage in this kind of destructiveness. It's understandable why I'd presume time to equal maturity, hoping my child's wisdom would increase gracefully with age; yet, I know many parents who live in daily bewilderment at the foolish choices of their grown children. The potential for poor judgment (especially in the face of temptation) knows no bounds—even with age or experience on our side.

Whether young or grown, child or parent, we all succumb to real and present dangers lurking in the shadows: the deceiving aroma of the Devil's allure. Regardless of the earthly wisdom we may gain over the years, only the power and wisdom we receive from the Holy Spirit offers a tangible battle strategy for overcoming temptation. Just as it took practice and time for our babies to learn how to walk without stumbling, likewise it takes time for us to learn how to walk by the Spirit with the mind of a conqueror.

WASHING WITH THE WORD

What keeps the Lord from scorning and condemning his children of their habitual, often flagrant transgressions? Shouldn't we know better by now, having experienced the bitter fruits of our deeds so many times before? Why does it seem like no matter how hard we try to control ourselves, sin keeps knocking at the door? For the answers, we must run to the gospel of truth and grace.

For I know that nothing good dwells in me, that is, in my flesh. For I have the desire to do what is right but not the ability to carry it out. For I do not do the good I want, but the evil I do not want I keep on doing. Romans 7:18–19 ESV

As the apostle Paul confessed in this passage, though we may desire to do right with our heads, the wars raging within our messy hearts can inhibit our ability to do so. Paul voices his personal grief over this clash in v. 15 (ESV), "For I do not understand my own actions. For I do not do what I want, but I do the very thing that I hate."

The "very thing that I hate" Paul is referring to is *sin*, and when the Bible mentions sin, it speaks of "missing the mark."[2]

If even the apostles struggled to hit the target of perfection every time, why would we expect any different for ourselves? King Solomon addressed this bleak reality when he wrote, "Indeed, there is *no one* on earth who is righteous, *no one* who does what is right and never sins." (Ecclesiastes 7:20 NIV, emphasis mine)

Yet, there is an ointment of hope in this passage that we should apply to our aching souls. Having the mind of Christ (1 Corinthians 2:12–16) means that we, like Paul, can confess the very things we hate are also the very sins we pray to be cleansed from. If God had not given us this renewed mind, we would be ignorant of our sin struggle in the first place. We hate the war within us because we now see sin for all its bad fruits and shame (Romans 6:20–23). This recognition is a good thing, made possible only by the Spirit of God dwelling within us.

The space between the desire to do right and the ability to do right is a gap the Spirit helps close during our walk with Christ. Still, the best news we can hear after acknowledging repeated personal shortcomings is this: Christ filled the requirement of "do-right" perfection more than 2,000 years ago on our behalf. That is why Paul rejoices in Romans 7:24–25, "Wretched man that I am! Who will deliver me from this body of death? Thanks be to God through Jesus Christ our Lord!"

We know that our old sinful selves were crucified with Christ so that sin might lose its power in our lives. We are no longer slaves to sin. Romans 6:6 NLT

When Christ was crucified, so were we. Not in the physical sense of the word, but in the spiritual sense. The crucifixion was not only the greatest apex of agony in human history, but also the very place where our greatest victory was won (1 Corinthians 15:57).

Christ's sacrifice makes it possible for us to approach the throne of grace in our time of need (Hebrews 4:16), and his triumph over death means that we have died to sin and received new life (Romans 6:11). Having been freed from the chains of transgression, we are given power by the Holy Spirit to overcome temptation. In Christ, we are *instantly* a new creation (2 Corinthians 5:17), but we are *not instantly* conformed into his likeness. Thus, discouragement can abound when we feel we're not living as righteously as we should or could be.

A portion of this battle has to do with belief: do we really believe God when he says we are no longer slaves to sin? Have our old sinful selves *really* been nailed to the cross with Christ? The unchanging and unfailing word of Scripture says we've been freed, but our unstable and unruly emotions attempt to suggest otherwise. It is at this crossroad Satan appears, delighting to plant seeds of doubt which call our eternal allegiance into question. This is the fight for which scripture advises us to unsheathe "the sword of the Spirit, which is the word of God." (Ephesians 6:17 ESV)

The word of the cross is the power of God to overcome death *and* temptation (1 Corinthians 1:18). In the fight between Spirit and flesh, the power of the cross can be made manifest as a weapon against sinful urges. Even if we have not managed to memorize a single verse of scripture, as believers we do know with confidence the "word of the cross:" Jesus paid the price to set us free from our bondage to sin and conquered Satan and death by rising again. The simple power of this truth, when proclaimed by the lips of God's son or daughter, is big enough to slay Satan's evil enticements. By God's grace, we're free to say "yes" to righteousness, for sin no longer has dominion over us (Romans 6.13–14).

The temptations in your life are no different from what others experience. And God is faithful. He will not allow the temptation to be more than you can stand. When you are tempted, he will show you a way out so that you can endure. 1 Corinthians 10:13 NLT

Our training in the Spirit leads to an increased obedience to God's Word and sensitivity to his direction. One of the reasons I've struggled with habitual sin so frequently is simply (yet rather embarrassingly) because I refused to listen to the Spirit's promptings. If the Helper sounds the alarm when we've wandered off path and tells us how to redirect our steps (Isaiah 11:2), the question then becomes whether or not we will humble ourselves enough to obey.

The problem isn't that our struggles are too big or obscure. God says the temptations we face are not uncommon to man and that he will always provide a path of escape. The real problem is we don't always have the courage to trust his leading. We don't always believe the "way out" he provides is good enough. I'm sure many of us do hear the Spirit's coaching when we're presented with the chance to turn from sin, but for one reason or another, our pride convinces us to ignore him (Galatians 5:17).

I can state this point boldly because I'm guilty of such redundant folly. When I'm upset about the actions or words of others, I justify my own sinful responses because I feel I'm "in the right." Oh, how extremely difficult it is to be humble when I believe I'm the one being wronged! Even still, those are precisely the times the Spirit is teaching me to cling to God's sovereignty,[3] knowing that he fights battles on my behalf (Exodus 14:14) and gives abundant grace to those who humble themselves rather than act proudly in their own defense (James 4:6).

Trusting that God is our ultimate satisfaction and champion is directly related to our grounding in God's Word and abiding in the Vine (John 15:5). We've been given all the tools required to turn away from sin—we need only plug into the power source of Christ through *fellowship, prayer, and meditation*[4] (Romans 15:1–6). Eradicating sinful habits from our heart will not happen in solitary confinement. Instead, it should be a community effort requiring the power and wisdom of the Holy Trinity working through the counsel of other faithful believers in our lives.

As we confess to each other the sin-stained tendencies we struggle with, the Spirit gives us the horsepower needed to steer toward a different direction (James 5:16). Over time, we begin to cry to the Lord to reroute us off the rocky roads of temptation (Psalm 19:13). And, as a good Father should, his patient hand leads us away from the dead ends of perpetual transgressions to a more faithful and fruitful horizon. Though we may lose battles from time to time in our struggle against sin, we certainly do not lose our heavenly hope. The good news of Christ gives us the courage to endure, the grace to fail, and the mercy to receive another chance.

BATHING IN PRAYER

Lord, you are the God who made a way for the Israelites to escape Egypt, and you are the same God who made a way for humanity to be reconciled to your presence. There is nothing impossible for you to accomplish, not even the purging of sin from my heart. God, I appeal to your mercy, as I know many times I have made wrong choices, turning away from opportunities to make right ones. You have offered me

17

deliverance from temptation, but foolishly I have refused out of arrogance and ignorance. I cry to you now to take pity on my weak and fallen flesh, so I may know what it is to live by the Spirit you have put within me. Lead me to paths of righteousness and keep me from the traps of the Evil One, who longs to see me fail once again. By your power and grace, I commit my steps to your perfect will. All glory and honor to you, amen.

HANGING HEARTS OUT TO DRY
STUDY REFLECTIONS

Read 1 Corinthians 10:13. Do you believe God remains faithful to help when you are tempted by sin? Build your confidence in this attribute of God by seeking three scriptures that speak to his faithfulness or his being faithful. Write the verses you find in your journal for quick reference in the future. (Tip: use your Bible's concordance to look up these keywords or search in your web browser by typing "Bible verse for God's faithfulness")

MEMORIZATION:

We know that our old sinful selves were crucified with Christ so that sin might lose its power in our lives. We are no longer slaves to sin. Romans 6:6 NLT

PRAYER:

Read Psalm 51:10. Use this psalm to write out your own prayer, asking God to increase your awareness of his Spirit when you are faced with a choice to sin or obey his leading. Confess sins that you struggle with habitually and ask for the faith to believe God's ways are more satisfying and fulfilling than the sins that deceive you.

**The Son of God could not meet
all the needs around him.**

He had to get away to pray. He had to eat. He had to
sleep. He had to say no. If Jesus had to live with human
limitations, we'd be foolish to think we don't. The
people on this planet who end up doing nothing are
those who never realized they couldn't do everything.[1]
Kevin DeYoung

3

The Poor Juggler

When I finally came back to earth, I realized I hadn't heard a word she said. Our daughter was rambling on about the day's events as we drove home from school, but I had completely zoned out. At some point I switched over to autopilot mode— safely navigating us home physically, yet nowhere to be found mentally. The anxious pacing in my mind had whisked me away in a whirlwind, thinking of tasks that waited to welcome me home.

As we turned the corner, I tried to snap out of it. I confessed I hadn't been paying attention and asked that she start over from the beginning. Without delay, she proceeded to recount the story with the same vigor as the first-time around. I felt myself strained to remain concentrated on what she had to share, knowing my cell phone contained urgent emails pending my reply. Determined to focus, I set down the electronic diversion and began to ask questions about her day, proving the attention I'd paid.

It's not an uncommon occurrence, this drifting off of mine. When the days are filled with too many tasks, it's usually because I've given permission to the overload. By labeling myself a "multi-tasker," I've accepted my ego-centric ability to get things done against all odds—regardless of the relationships gone neglected as a result.

THE MESSINESS OF BEING BUSY

As I later reflected upon my dismissive distraction toward our daughter, I wondered how greatly my self-inflicted busyness cost me in quality time with her over the years. As the Holy Spirit began to reveal the sour taste of my hurried pursuits, my heart became grieved over the lost moments of love, and ultimately, the joy I had let slip away. In my sorrowful rumination, he presented my multi-tasking in a way I'd never considered before.

Truth be told, juggling 20 proverbial balls at once leaves me joyless and stressed. Although I can multi-task quite efficiently, I've come to learn I ought not to do it at all. While it may appear that mile-high duties are the result of selfless service to others, I've grown to understand something different: my ego tends to benefit the most from my efforts while my loved ones benefit the least. It turns out I have been sacrificing the fruit of the Spirit (Galatians 5:22) on the altar of busyness, and it leaves my poor heart a bloody mess.

If we look to God's wisdom regarding the best way to best handle our time, we won't find instruction to do as many activities as we possibly can at the cost of our availability to love. Even though society sings the praises of mothers who can work, clean, care for the family, run the PTA, volunteer at pet shelters (and also look perfect while doing it), those of us trusting in the gospel for renewal and refreshment should take a longer look at this matter. In doing so, we may find that we've made ourselves busy because it makes us feel important and not because God has asked us to take up such a schedule.

The bottom line in this self-evaluation may be a kick in the head, but a necessary one. Have we traded what God says is necessary for what we believe is necessary when it comes to filling our time? Are we leaving behind the better things in order to accomplish the bulk of things?

WASHING WITH THE WORD

The Bible is not a book of rules to follow in order to obtain God's blessing; grace ensures that we cannot boast in our ability to comply with the rules to earn favor (Ephesians 2:8–9). Likewise, the Bible does not specifically address how to spend every hour of our time on earth. Those of us who work well with checklists may find this a bit disappointing at first, since we're often rule-following perfectionists who like the feeling of accomplishment and compliance (or perhaps that's just me).

As we look at the Scriptures together, however, we begin to see God's guidance concerning our busyness often targets the *heart* behind the activity instead of the activity itself.

Good and upright is the LORD; therefore he instructs sinners in his ways. Psalm 25:8 NIV

The first thing we must consider here is how God's goodness[2] and righteousness gives discernment to his people—leading to wisdom on how to divvy up our time. Through the disobedience of Adam and Eve came separation between God and man, but through the obedience of Christ came the opportunity for reconciliation between the two (Romans 5:15). This reconciliation would be impossible if it weren't for the goodness and righteousness of God. By devising a plan for the relationship between sinner and Savior to be renewed, God is able to speak directly to his people through his Word to instruct, correct, and train us in holiness (2 Timothy 3:16).

Thanks to the perfect life, death, and resurrection of Jesus Christ, God was able to tear down the walls of the great divide and reestablish lines of communication directly to the hearts of his people, instead of the Old Testament method of revelation through prophets and kings (Matthew 27:51). Since he is good and upright, and because of the completed work of Christ,[4] he is able to write his commandments on our hearts to show us his honorable ways (Jeremiah 31:33). This divine illumination of God's will for the day means we can surrender our expectations and embrace his interruptions without getting defensive or bitter. The Lord's instruction gives peace to our hearts, not because his will is bending to ours, but because we're surrendering our schedules to higher and better ways (Isaiah 55:9).

*He has told you, O man, what is good; and what does
the Lord require of you but to do justice, and to love kindness,
and to walk humbly with your God?* Micah 6:8 ESV

When the Lord communicates his ways, he constantly stresses the first two commandments: to love God and love our neighbors as ourselves. Jesus reiterated that the entire Law of God rested upon these two commands (Matthew 22:40). He doesn't itemize everything we are supposed to be doing throughout our day, but he does give us a baseline of attitudes and actions for our own good, for the good of others, and for the good news to be spread around the world.

With this in mind, we should ask ourselves: *do our hectic schedules make us better lovers of God and people?* Personally, I struggle to love well when I'm stressed and overburdened with tasks, even if those tasks are for good purposes. I grow snappy, grumpy and a host of other adjectives that could double as names for Snow White's seven dwarfs. In these instances, even my good works amount to nothing because the driving force is not my love for people, but rather my pride in accomplishing a goal, earning praise, or living up to the expectations of others (1 Corinthians 13:1–3).

God's reminder to do justice, love kindness, and walk humbly is a direct call to live out a life of love toward God and people in everything we do. If our busyness keeps us from training our hearts to love and serve the way he tells us to, we're missing out on the abundant life Christ came to give us (John 10:10), and also impeding the opportunity for witness[5] in our community.

"Martha, Martha," the Lord answered, "you are worried and upset about many things, but few things are needed— or indeed only one. Mary has chosen what is better, and it will not be taken away from her." Luke 10:41–42 NIV

We'd be remiss not to take a look at this exchange, especially as busy moms. If you aren't familiar with this verse in Luke 10, I would encourage you to read it on your own to better understand the context. However, the condensed version is that Mary and Martha were sisters, Martha was a busy-body preparing an enormous feast for a house full of guests and she was upset that her sister wasn't helping (Luke 10:40). Instead, Mary was sitting at the feet of Jesus, listening to him speak (Luke 10:39).

Mary had chosen the better activity for the moment, instead of joining the hustle of trying to impress everyone with admirable multi-tasking capabilities. Martha was busy making much of her home and her dinner, while Mary was busy making much of the time she had in the presence of the Lord. Where Martha could only see her performance, Mary could only see her relationship to Christ.

Martha isn't a bad woman for her desire to put on the perfect dinner. In fact, the Bible speaks of the importance of good hospitality as a way to demonstrate our love for others (Romans 12:13). However, this account between sisters shows us exactly where the Lord wants our hearts to be in the midst of the everyday whirlwinds. He doesn't want our hopes set on the things we need to do in our daily routine, especially when it causes us to be anxious or unloving. Rather, our Father wants our hearts and hopes set on keeping our relationship with Christ at the center, working for the Lord and not merely for the praises of those around us (Colossians 3:23–24).

With the Spirit's help, we can pray for the underlying reasons of our busyness to be revealed (i.e. to feel important, accepted, valuable, desired, included, successful, etc.), and the wisdom to know where cutbacks need to be made. If it's changed hearts we're after, we must follow the will of the Lord instead of the will of our overextended commitments. The former wants only our good, but the latter may well keep us from it.

BATHING IN PRAYER

Father I praise you, for from the beginning of time you have laid a foundation that has set my path before you. You have brought me to this difficult moment where I must stare at my heart to see where I have pushed what you treasure away. I confess my focus is more on my desire to accomplish tasks than to bask in the light of what your Son has finished on the cross. Lord, I get so trapped by the praises of men and my pride that I have chosen to occupy myself with things that are not the better portion. Heal me of my need to be seen as a magnificent multi-tasker, and instead make the desire of my heart to dwell at the feet of my magnificent Savior. Show me where I can replace selfish pursuits with righteous endeavors, where your name is lifted high and all glory is bestowed to you. Only your Spirit can makes these changes in my heart, so I humbly bow down, ready and willing to hear his instruction. In Jesus' holy and perfect name, we pray all these things, amen.

HANGING HEARTS OUT TO DRY
STUDY REFLECTIONS

Read Jeremiah 17:7–8 & John 15:4–5. Mary chose to spend time at the feet of Jesus, listening to him teach. This time is precious for us also, playing an important part in our spiritual growth. Based on reading the verses in Jeremiah and John, why do you think time with Jesus should be the best, most important part of our schedules?

MEMORIZATION

He has told you, O man, what is good; and what does the Lord require of you but to do justice, and to love kindness, and to walk humbly with your God? Micah 6:8 ESV

PRAYER

Read Psalm 25:8. Listed below are some main ways God uses to instruct us in his ways. Consider how much time you spend weekly allowing God to counsel you through these methods and circle the ones you'd like to pray about improving. Write a prayer in your journal making a petition for improved commitment and obedience in these areas.

- ° Praying
- ° Reading the Bible
- ° Hearing the Word preached
- ° Fellowshipping with other believers
- ° Singing/listening to worship music

To flee from God is to rise against God.

Every time we sin, we're telling God, "My way of navigating
this particular situation is better than yours. My wisdom
and skill are more efficient and more effective in this
moment than your wisdom and skill." It's not that we
stop believing. It's just that what we believe has shifted.[1]
Tullian Tchividjian

4

Return to Me

Sprinting in flip-flops is a hazardous risk, but I had no choice since the situation escalated so quickly. When I told our toddler son it was time to leave the park we were playing at, he replied eagerly, "Okay, Mom!" The quick compliance fooled me only briefly.

At the fork in the sidewalk, we split; I headed toward the car pushing my baby girl in her stroller as my boy tip-toed atop the blue handicap paint on the curb. Slowly, he started heading down the sidewalk, picking up confidence and speed with every stride.

"Stop!" I shouted, "Come back to Mom!"

I waited to make a move, dividing my gaze between the stroller and the running renegade. He stopped just long enough for me to watch the wheels spinning inside of his blonde sweaty head. The temptation proved to be too strong for his two-year-old psyche, so he took off running away down the parking lot sidewalk.

THE MESSINESS OF RUNNING

I continued to plea for his return, but to no avail. Not once did he stop to look back, even though I could tell from his giggling he could hear me. I quickly decided the fidgeting baby in the stroller would have to wait while I put my flip-flops to work as running shoes. I darted towards him while yelling for his attention, but he only ran faster, intensifying the danger by nearly entering the parking lot full of cars coming and going. I'm not sure which was a bigger hit to my pride: that I had to run quite ungraciously to snatch him up 12 cars down the lot, or that he completely ignored my cries to return safely to me.

With every smack of my sandal slapping the ground, I began to see the situation from a new perspective. As I watched our son run away, I realized what I must look like during my rebellious attempts to flee from the Lord. However, I also began to better understand God's pursuit of me when I'm caught up in reckless abandon.

God used this display of our son's disobedience to reflect something of my own, as well as to open my eyes to the heartbreak he feels when his beloved children prefer running towards danger instead of his assurance. Toddlers aren't the only ones gifted at sprinting in wrong directions. Deep in our core, we too sense this knowledge of running away from someone important—namely, our Creator.

WASHING WITH THE WORD

There comes a point when dealing with the choice rebellion of our children that we are forced to consider both perspectives: that of the runner and that of the Lord. It isn't until the Spirit places us in the mindset of both parties that we begin to see our tendencies as harmful, unwise, and an outright rejection of our relationship with God. Our messy hearts are natural-born runners, which is why we need Jesus' deliverance matched with the Spirit's power of reorientation. The good news of the gospel is the map that guides us in the proper direction.

"Meanwhile, the older son was in the fields working. When he returned home, he heard music and dancing in the house, and he asked one of the servants what was going on. 'Your brother is back,' he was told, 'and your father has killed the fattened calf. We are celebrating because of his safe return.'"
Luke 15:25–27 NLT

In recalling the parable of the prodigal son (Luke 15), many of us can relate to the journey of the wayward younger brother who ran away from his father and squandered his inheritance, only to come back filthy, poor, and repentant. Still, our running from God isn't always so obvious because our hearts can be deceitful. Few of us would think of the older son (who supposed his obedience would earn the reward of inheritance) as equally prone to running as his foolish brother (Luke 15:28–30). In both instances, these sons were darting away from the grace of their father, albeit one physically and the other emotionally. Neither son had a right heart toward their father, for both of them underestimated his grace and love.

In examining the relationships in this story, we see one son who wants to go his own way, one son who wants to earn his own way, and one father who graciously gives, either way. The older brother hadn't realized that everything belonging to his father was already his (Luke 15:31), and the younger brother hadn't expected to receive his dad's warm compassion upon his return (Luke 15:20). With some perspective, we begin to see parts of ourselves in each character of the story. We know what it's like to run rebelliously toward selfish pursuits. All of us, at one time or another, have attempted to earn merits with God in order to guarantee grace and blessing. And though we're well-versed in being stubborn children of God, our experiences as parents have taught us the delight of clenching a lost child returned from their wandering.

I have swept away your sins like a cloud. I have scattered your offenses like the morning mist. Oh, return to me, for I have paid the price to set you free. Isaiah 44:22 NLV

The flip-flop incident in the parking lot opened my eyes to what it may feel like when the Lord watches his children flee from his protection. Here in Isaiah 44, we hear an impassioned plea straight from the Father's lips, prefaced with a gospel proclamation: a way back to his arms has already been paved.

Is there a stronger urge we have as parents than protecting our children from hardship and pain? Much of the time spent raising little ones is wrought with keeping them safe and away from danger. We imagine one day we'll be thanked for the countless sacrifices it takes to raise a human from infancy to adulthood, but there's never a guarantee that appreciation will come. The Lord knows this risk of unreciprocated parental love—he taught Israel to walk, held him, healed him, fed him and loved him, yet the more he was called to return, the more he continued to go away (Hosea 11:1–4).

Our son wasn't heeding my warnings in the parking lot that day. He had no clue about the horrific dangers that awaited a decision to carelessly dart out into the busy roadway. However, I knew the potential for catastrophe, and his safest option was to stop and turn around. Even though he wasn't listening to me, I continued to wildly chase him like only a panicked mother hen could.

Similarly, the Lord continues to pursue us in our ignorance, not contented to watch us perish under the weight of holy judgment (2 Peter 3:9). It's as if he's tailing after us with a newspaper, waiving it in the air and shouting, "It is finished! I took care of it all! We can be together again, so stop running and let me show you what I did!" (John 3:16)

The good news of the gospel is the *headline* on that newspaper. God's fatherly delight is to boast in his completed plan of total reconciliation because it brings him glory *and* brings us safely home (Luke 15:10). Our sins can be swept away like a cloud because they were put upon the shoulders of Christ (John 1:29). We have been declared righteous and worthy because Jesus' life is credited to us the moment we confess him as Lord and Savior (Romans 10:9). In Christ alone our hope is found, because it is through his spilt blood we are made white as snow (1 John 1:7). My friends, there is no better kind of news—it's the truth that God continues to beckon us home with.

Has all of our running ever found us a greater consolation than the living hope we have in Jesus? The reason the Lord continues to go after our messy hearts is because he knows apart from him, we are not safe (Psalm 4:8). Listen to the love of the Father in this verse as he longs for you to embrace his grace once more: *"Oh, return to me, for I have paid the price to set you free."*

> *Let us test and examine our ways, and return*
> *to the Lord!* Lamentations 3:40 ESV

What is to be learned by admitting our tendencies to dart away from our heavenly Father? *There is hope for the chronic runner in all of us.* And while this living hope comes from the singular source of Christ, it must be fanned aflame by a community of believers who are strong in the Spirit and anchored in the Word of God. The body of Christ plays a vital role in examining past rebellions and the subsequent collateral damage (spiritual, emotional, physical, and mental) that results from going our own ways. Since testing our reasons for running will often produce a flood of convictions hidden under piles of guilt, it's not designed to be performed strictly in solitude.

In fact, it's impossible to fully examine our ways on our own, for isolation is a device of the enemy used to inoculate us with futility. As long as we believe we can be both patient *and* physician, we will continue to fumble over remedies that aren't ours to prescribe. Confessing our disobedience to fellow believers is the act that opens the door to healing and redirection (James 5:16). Bringing our rebellion to the light through fellowship with one another is the way the Holy Spirit works to purge unrighteousness from our hearts and reorient us to the Father (1 John 1:7).

Lamentations 3:40 is an invitation to return to the light, which is always the right direction. In doing so, the Holy Spirit helps us recognize where the fruits of frivolous pursuits have gone sour. Once we enter into agreement that our running has gotten us nowhere fast, our wandering hearts return to the Lord quicker than our feet can carry us. Out of love and gratitude, we sprint back to his arms—because he asks us to (Zechariah 1:3), because he cares for us (1 Peter 5:6–7), and because he longs for us to take his faithfulness seriously (Jeremiah 3:12).

Over time we can sense the Spirit strengthening a force in our heart, inclining us to about-face toward God the more we learn about his grace and forgiveness. As we taste and see that he is good (Psalm 34:8), we slow down to hear him offer a heavenly peace we'd never find on the run. Wearing flip-flops or running shoes, our direction makes all the difference.

BATHING IN PRAYER:

Father, you have gathered me into your fold and given me shelter. You are a wise and loving Shepherd who graciously tends to his flock. You have made every effort to make your love known, yet somehow it isn't always real to me. Lord, I confess the pride I carry when I am running from your grace or your love. It's impossible for me to have all the answers, and yet I continue to search for them without seeking you first. I ask that you open my eyes to see you at work in my life. Reveal to me your presence in all things, big or small. Consume my heart with your comfort so I can fully rest in the knowledge that my running cannot separate me from your love. Whom do I have in heaven but you, Lord? May I learn to run into your arms instead of away! Bless your holy and perfect name, amen.

HANGING HEARTS OUT TO DRY

STUDY REFLECTIONS

Read Lamentations 3:40. Our tendency to run from God can arise from feeling overly proud or confident in our own abilities. Learn more about what God's Word has to say about our pride by looking up three Scriptures on the topic. Write the verses you find in your journal for quick reference in the future. (Tip: use your Bible's concordance to look up this keyword or use your web browser and type "Bible verse for pride")

MEMORIZATION

I have swept away your sins like a cloud. I have scattered your offenses like the morning mist. Oh, return to me, for I have paid the price to set you free. Isaiah 44:22 NLV

PRAYER

Read Luke 15:3–10. These parables affirm the joy that is celebrated in heaven each time a sinner repents and returns back to the Lord. Write a prayer that confesses your own personal running from God. Be sure to express thanks for his grace and love in constantly pursuing you, in spite of your fleeing.

**At the bottom of our beauty struggles
is "a fight for divine glory."**

The vain, confident woman and the insecure, depressed
woman both want God's glory for themselves…
when we understand that our self-focus and vanity
is worse than we thought—robbing God of glory—
then we can take steps of repentance and experience
freedom from our struggles with beauty.[1]
Carolyn Mahaney & Nicole Whitacre

5

The Braiding of Hair

It hurt my feelings to hear she didn't like it, but even more that she said it was ugly. I had painstakingly parted each section of hair to make sure unruly fly-aways had been tamed. During her younger, more tangled years, taking a brush to our daughter's hair was a terrifying chore, to say the least. But having matured in her self-care capabilities, she was now able to brush her golden locks on her own to present me a mane prepped for my mediocre styling competence.

Over the years, my ability to execute more sophisticated techniques has grown steadily, though I'll admit my skills have peaked at the french-braid pigtail design. Nevertheless, my heart still beams with pride every time she lets me weave her thick wavy blondness into something that comes across as an embrace of femininity—even when she's wearing her black skater high tops.

This particular morning, there was a greater necessity for careful grooming. Our growing fourth grader was running for Vice President at her elementary school and scheduled to give a campaign speech in front of her classmates. Assuming the position of her campaign fashion consultant, I orchestrated a clean, coordinated outfit and classic hairstyle to match. French-braid pigtails seemed a natural choice for such an important occasion.

THE MESSINESS OF PERCEPTIONS

I knew she looked as beautiful as ever, but she saw herself through some grouchy morning eye-boogers that terribly blurred her vision. She grunted and grimaced painfully in the mirror's reflection, totally rejecting what I thought looked lovely. Try as I might to convince her that the finished 'do was worth keeping, I gave her the option to make her own decision. Disappointed, I allowed her to walk away completely undone, even though it hurt my heart she didn't see the same reflection of elegance that I did.

As a parent, I felt saddened she didn't trust my opinion, but as a woman, I knew first-hand the complications of self-acceptance. I frequently pair a heavy sigh with a furrowed brow, dwelling on my impression of physical inadequacy. Especially after having children (and in my case, back-to-back babies), the constant onslaught of negative thinking is enough to drive me into a pit of self-loathing and disgust.

We often gaze into the mirror, recalling all the beauty we think we've lost due to the passing of time or the rearing of babes, not considering the meticulous effort God put into making us beautiful in his sight. Instead, we critique and pinch ourselves in all the right places of squishy excess, unknowingly accusing God of getting us all wrong.

WASHING WITH THE WORD

Our hearts can get so caught up in the skinny jeans that no longer fit that we forget about the robe of righteousness Christ adorns us with. When reflections in the mirror dominate our thoughts, it's time to reflect upon our hearts' focus: are we fixed upon God's unchanging truth, or have we found ourselves tripping over temporary troubles? Drowning in self-pity as a result of staring at the mirror serves to validate our desperation for rescue. Keeping us afloat in the raging sea of discontent is the Holy Spirit, sent to remind us about eternal realities which don't ebb and flow along with the tide or the scale (John 16:13).

I am overwhelmed with joy in the Lord my God! For he has dressed me with the clothing of salvation and draped me in a robe of righteousness. I am like a bridegroom dressed for his wedding or a bride with her jewels. Isaiah 61:10 NLT

Like a bride and groom dressed for their wedding is the woman and man adorned by the Lord. How often do you feel that way when you wake up in the morning?

Although we don't typically see ourselves in this light, God wants our joy and satisfaction to rest upon enduring truths— not in our physical appearance or flashy wardrobe, but rather in the gospel with which he fashions us. As Isaiah rejoices in this verse, he proclaims that receiving the salvation of the Lord is the same as being dressed for the best day of his life. The trials, the aches, the aging, and brokenness will be but a small blip on the radar in comparison with the celebration we've been made ready for (Isaiah 62:4–5)

This may not mean much as we struggle for joy here-and-now because our standards remain worldly in so many ways (1 Corinthians 3:3). If this is the case, then we should be asking ourselves what we have placed our faith in. Have we cast our hopes upon our ability to look youthful and untouched by the hands of time, or is our ultimate confidence in a resurrected Savior who has come to make all things new (Revelation 21:5)? Are we spending more time seeking glory and praise for our physical beauty than we are glorifying the beauty of the Lord (Psalm 27:4)?

I realize how difficult it is to battle negative self-image, and I certainly don't pretend to scratch the surface of the topic here in this book. I do aim, however, to drag us toward the indelible hope we can set anchor in (Hebrews 6:19). By planting our assurances in God's concrete promises instead of fickle human notions, our confidence shifts from what is seen to what is unseen yet hoped for (2 Corinthians 4:18), and from what fades to what stands forever (Isaiah 40:8). Turning our focus toward the radiant beauty of God's grace as depicted in the gospel, and artistry as demonstrated in creation, provides more than enough food for healthier thoughts.

God's infallible Word affirms his gaze pierces straight to our hearts, bypassing whatever beauty we're able to superficially present to the world (1 Samuel 16:7). Keeping all of these truths in mind, we can be sure that a heart bound to Christ is the most beautiful thing in the world; even better, it produces an eternal beauty which remains untouched by the passage of time.

You are altogether beautiful, my love; there is no flaw in you. Song of Solomon 4:7 ESV

This verse sounds like something you'd hear in a movie scene where two swooning lovers are doting over one another, but in fact these are God's very words to us. Perhaps we've never enjoyed such delightful affirmation, at least not with such simplistic linguistic elegance. The truth is, even if we did hear this statement from our loved ones, chances are slim we'd believe it to be uttered sincerely, without an ulterior motive or element of pacification.

Do you believe that in Christ, there is no flaw in you? That you are altogether beautiful? These words are from a God who does not lie (1 Samuel 15:29). Dare we deny his authentic adoration, especially since it cost him so dearly to express it? True, sin has caused us to grow jaded in genuinely receiving esteem such as this, but let's remember the bigger picture: it costs nothing for a human to whisper these sweet nothings into your ear, yet it cost the Lord *everything* to be able to do so. What more must he do to prove his words are sincere when he exclaims, "Behold, you are beautiful, my love, behold you are beautiful!" (Song of Solomon 4:1)?

We once were stained and unfit for a seat at the table, but in Christ we are made to be co-heirs[2] (Romans 8:17). Because the robe of Christ's righteousness covers us, we are seen as perfect in the sight of the Lord (Colossians 1:22). The gospel makes us something we could never have been on our own: totally and completely lovely to God. And at the end of it all, to whom else must we appear lovely? Ultimately, there's only one perspective that counts for anything in eternity: the Lord's.

But who are you, O man, to answer back to God?
Will what is molded say to its molder, "Why have
you made me like this?" Romans 9:20 ESV

I often drown in self-consciousness, so this verse tends to be a good kick in the pants for when I'm really picking myself apart. When I stare into the mirror wishing away my uncooperative wavy hair, the Spirit answers me back with this question. Perhaps you obsess over bushy eyebrows, thin lips, a double chin, or some other sort of feature that plagues you with revulsion. Whatever it is, whether you were born with it or it developed over time, God created you uniquely to experience his design for your life—warts and all. Even our flaws play a part in the Lord's mission to transform our hearts; he uses them to show us where we're clinging to temporal things more tightly than the Almighty himself (Proverbs 31:30).

We live in a fallen world corrupted by the curse of disease and death. There are aspects of the Fall that will weigh on our mortal bodies, such as wrinkles, white hairs, and chin whiskers (2 Corinthians 4:16). But every now and then, we need this arresting conviction from Romans to remind us that dissatisfaction with our physical attributes can lead to an accusation of the Lord's craftsmanship and care.

These reminders from Scripture aren't solely for our benefit; we would do well to also encourage our children in these truths (Isaiah 54:13). They may not believe our compliments because of some perceived parental obligation to spout them, but by teaching these assurances as trustworthy and true, we preach to their hearts and ours all the more. Building foundations upon identity and acceptance in Christ instead of appearance means time or temperament will not shake their confidence, or ours (Isaiah 28:16).

In fits of overwhelming frustration, when all the places we supposedly fall short in our beauty are magnified, let us call upon the Spirit to combat the taunts of the Evil One with the word of our Beloved in heaven. A heart turned towards him, no matter how messy, is always transformed into something royally exquisite (Isaiah 62:3). And that, dear sister, is beauty you can't buy off the shelf.

BATHING IN PRAYER

Our Lord, our Beloved, our Maker, there is none who compares to you. You have made me uniquely in your image, and for that I am amazed and overjoyed. But Father, as I pour out my desperate heart, I confess that I have gawked at my many faults instead of gazing at your Son's perfections. Help me Lord, for my failing flesh and withering beauty are not what you covet. Heal my heart from my own silly standards of beauty and protect it from the harsh opinions of the world around me. Open my eyes, Lord, so I can see myself how you see me in Christ. May my face shine with the beautiful glory that comes from being in your presence. In your perfect name we pray, amen.

HANGING OUR HEARTS OUT TO DRY
STUDY REFLECTIONS

Read Song of Solomon 4:7. Though a short verse, it speaks volumes to how God views us in Christ. Because of Jesus, God sees us in a variety of wonderful ways. Practice affirming these truths to yourself by writing out the following lines and filling in the blank with your name. Note the coordinating Bible verse that confirms these truths.

Example: "You are altogether beautiful, <u>Christine</u>; there is no flaw in you."

   1.) You are altogether beautiful, ＿＿＿＿＿＿＿＿; there is no flaw in you (Song of Solomon 4:7).

2.) You are altogether righteous, _____; there is no flaw in you (2 Corinthians 5:21).

3.) You are altogether accepted, _____; there is no flaw in you (Romans 5:17).

4.) You are altogether precious, _____; there is no flaw in you (Proverbs 3:15).

5.) You are altogether pure, _____; there is no flaw in you (Matthew 5:8).

MEMORIZATION

But who are you, O man, to answer back to God? Will what is molded say to its molder, "Why have you made me like this?" Romans 9:20 ESV

PRAYER

Read Isaiah 61:10. Overwhelming joy in the Lord can be the result of remembering the dire condition we were in before we came into a relationship with Christ. Take some time to write out a prayer of praise and adoration for the Lord, recalling all of his wondrous deeds. Affirm who he is, what he has done for you, and the joy that comes from knowing that your future in eternity has been secured through the life, death, and resurrection of his Son. Compare this eternal joy to the lack of joy you might be struggling with regarding your appearance or physical condition. Ask the Spirit to keep your heart set on Christ instead of the mirror's reflection.

What does it matter if our own plans are frustrated?

Is it not better to serve our neighbor than to have our own way? Once a man has experienced the mercy of God in his life he will henceforth aspire only to serve. The proud throne of the judge no longer lures him; he wants to be down below with the lowly and the needy, because that is where God found him.[1]
Dietrich Bonhoeffer

6

Reluctant Hands

It was his second trip to the emergency room in less than 24 hours. In an apparent allergic reaction to the medication prescribed for tonsillitis the visit before, my husband returned to the hospital for urgent treatment and IV fluid. I dropped him off before picking up our eldest from school, and then headed home with the brood in tow, trying to wrap my brain around a dinner idea that might magically cook itself.

After slapping some semblance of a meal together, I began my mildly-obsessive routine of cleaning the house. I went above and beyond this time, knowing my husband was quite ill and contagious germs abounded. I tore off our bed sheets, removed pillow cases, and loaded the soiled linens into the washing machine. My sights were set on presenting a totally clean bedroom to my husband upon his recovered return. Who *doesn't want* to rest in a clean bedroom on freshly laundered sheets when they're feeling sick?

Realizing I could be called any moment to pick him up from the hospital, I enlisted our eldest daughter for help. Though aware of her dad's withered condition, her response was not the eager help I was hoping for.

THE MESSINESS OF HELPING

"I'm just *so* tired," she whined, "Why do we have to do this now?" Reflexively, I shot her *the look*—you know, the look moms carry around in their holster when they need children to tread lightly and comply quickly.

"Fine! Where are the paper towels?" she snapped in response to my piercing glare.

Immediately, I walked over to her, bent down to her eye level, and sternly informed her that help was unwanted if she was going to do it begrudgingly. After attempting to explain away her attitude with some grumbling, she pitched in with a lighter mood and buffed the dust off the nightstands like a pro.

In this instance of illness, I labored intently to serve the needs of my husband—but often this isn't the case. I struggle, as our daughter did, to keep a right attitude when helping my family with their oft ill-timed requests. Why does lending a helping hand to people outside of the home seem more effortless in comparison to the reluctant hands I have for serving under my roof? Can it truly be called service if we're only helping on our terms? Can it truly be called loving if we're only serving when convenient?

WASHING WITH THE WORD

The Lord calls us to selflessly sacrifice daily, inside and outside the home (Luke 9:23). Even as I write this, I'm embarrassed about my unwillingness to help the ones I love the most when I'm trapped inside my self-centered world. Can there be anything more difficult than leaving the "Christine-kingdom" I'm trying to build so I can join the mission God has commanded me with? When acts of service turn into bitter beasts of burden, it's time to check our hearts at the cross for a clearer view.

For we are God's handiwork, created in Christ Jesus to do good works, which God prepared in advance for us to do. Ephesians 2:10 NIV

I continue to return to the truths of creation because in our origins we find our purpose. Not only are we God's handiwork from natural human birth, but we're also a new creation when we are born again in Christ (2 Corinthians 5:17). It is God himself who brings these new beginnings to pass, and it is also the Lord who brings to completion the good works being done in and though us (Philippians 1:6).

Created to do good deeds for God's glory (Matthew 5:16)—the Commander-in-Chief has issued an executive order. With this awareness, I should wake up every morning and know that the main assignment for the day will be to *help other people.* Much to my chagrin, this is not the perspective I peel back the bed sheets back with. Even worse, when the Lord brings me opportunities to help my children or husband, I usually grumble about feeling inconvenienced.

Our Father knows how to help us walk in the good works he has laid before us; yet another reason he sent to us the Helper (Zechariah 4:6). Though the realities of this truth may appear mysterious to us, these deeds of service overflow out of our love for him—the more we fall in love with our Lord, the more we want to be used as instruments of blessing to others.

This Spirit-fueled desire does not put us on quest for mortal praise or esteem, but rather sets aflame the desire to be a reflection of God's love and service. Out of our overwhelming reverence and gratitude comes a desire to obey his commands and love others as ourselves. God makes it happen according to his perfect plan by planting the seed of obedience, keeping it watered, and helping it grow in order to bless those around us.

For you were called to freedom, brothers. Only do not use your freedom as an opportunity for the flesh, but through love serve one another. For the whole law is fulfilled in one word: "You shall love your neighbor as yourself." Galatians 5:13–14 ESV

God's grace can sometimes be viewed as scandalous because we cannot earn it *or* lose it; grace is completely independent of anything we may or may not do, which is why it is defined as *unmerited* favor. Some, who lean towards religiosity, think that salvation must be earned, proven, and/or maintained through works. Others, who have a false view of grace, believe the phrase, "Jesus paid it all" really means, "Behave however you'd like and Jesus will pick up the tab." Neither of these views properly accept the free gift of grace in Jesus Christ (Ephesians 2:8–9), and neither view will generate a right heart attitude when serving our fellow man—for either one will serve out of self-righteousness or out of self-aggrandizement.

The Bible is full of beautiful paradoxes that, to the outsider, seem to be nonsensical. Having been bought with a price *does* give us a freedom we've never known before, and learning how to live within its boundaries that can be very confusing. Doesn't that seem like opposing ideas: freedom with boundaries?

The Spirit helps us stare more intently into our redeemed hearts, bringing into clear focus the blessing of this apparent contradiction. Those who have experienced Jesus Christ breaking the chains of sin and addiction in their lives know first-hand what it is to really be "free" (John 8:36). They know the boundaries God sets are not restrictive, but are required for authentic and abundant life in Christ. The Lord isn't keeping us from something good by giving us limits within our freedom. He is giving us his immeasurable goodness by offering the gift of grace he paid for so dearly (Romans 6:22–23).

Therefore, freedom in Christ does not mean freedom to do as you please, and Jesus reminds us others will know we're truly disciples by the love we show for one another (John 13:35), especially in their time of need. As we continue to abide in Christ and let his Word dwell in us richly (Colossians 3:16), we use the freedom he has earned for us to serve the needs of others, and not primarily our self-interests (Philippians 2:4).

God is not unjust; he will not forget your work and the love you have shown him as you have helped his people and continue to help them. Hebrews 6:10 NIV

I don't usually equate serving others to be the same as serving the Lord, at least not under my family's roof. It is easier to see my efforts as a work unto the Lord when I'm out of the house and serving in ministry. Yet when Scripture says as we do to each other we also do to the Lord (Matthew 25:40), it makes no distinction for location or blood relation. Showing love for others through helping hands—whether inside or outside the home—counts as honoring the Lord in your body (1 Corinthians 6:19–20), and this he will reward generously (Galatians 6:9).

We help our children with their homework—so too, we are helping God. We ignore the needs of others to serve our own desires—so too, we ignore God and the opportunity to be his hands and feet[2] in a hurting world.

God's Word highlights Jesus' willing service, but also exalts his willing sacrifice. Service can indeed exist without sacrifice, but God's kingdom calls emphatically for both. Though his example is higher than we can mimic perfectly in this life, the Spirit enables increased selflessness here and now, for God's glory and our hearts' transformation. When the Lord gives us opportunities to put our hands to good deeds (*especially* for blessing those we live with), may we look to the cross, take a deep breath, and let the Spirit have his way to work through us.

BATHING IN PRAYER

Heavenly Father, thank you for sending Jesus to demonstrate sacrificial service in all of its beauty. We know that his perfect life of surrender and sufficient death on the cross are the reasons we can boldly approach you in prayer. Lord, we grow weary of the constant demands on our time and the call to serve our families so tirelessly. We confess our bitterness grows when we feel unappreciated and exasperated. We know this is not your will. God, please breathe new life into us as we turn toward you, surrendering our selfishness in these moments. Remind us that you have promised to be our strength and our joy when we feel we cannot gladly serve. We humbly ask for your grace to overpower our emotions so we can learn how to live and to love through the giving of ourselves. In the name of Jesus Christ, amen.

HANGING HEARTS OUT TO DRY
STUDY REFLECTION

Read 1 Peter 4:10 & John 13:12–14. Based on these Scriptures and what you've read in this chapter, what does it mean when God commands you to love your neighbor as yourself?

MEMORIZATION

For we are God's handiwork, created in Christ Jesus to do good works, which God prepared in advance for us to do. Ephesians 2:10 NIV

PRAYER

Read Hebrews 6:10. How have you been challenged in this chapter to welcome interruptions as a chance to bring glory to God through your service? Write a prayer to the Lord thanking him for giving us Jesus, the ultimate example of what it means to love selflessly. Confess any hardness of heart you feel when it comes to helping your family with their needs and ask for the Spirit's help to become increasingly obedient in this area.

**The fear of God is the corner
stone of all blessedness.**

It is idle to talk of fearing the Lord if we act like those who
have no care whether there be a God or no, God's ways will
be our ways if we have a sincere reverence for him: if the
heart is joined unto God, the feet will follow hard after him.[1]
Charles H. Spurgeon

7

Half-Hearted Fear

Her back-talk had crossed the line. Heaven help us, we can barely keep up with the slings and arrows when she's moved past the point of no return with irritation. I recall behaving in this manner to a much milder degree when I was her age (or maybe that's just how I'd like to remember it), but the Lord had different plans for our daughter's temper when he matched my DNA with that of my husband.

The fiery storm of wailing toddlers and complicated math homework birthed an eruption of frustration out of her gut. Upset she couldn't concentrate due to the noisy surroundings, she lashed out to everyone within earshot about how her studies were being incessantly hindered.

Though we had tried to talk her off the ledge, she was caught up in a whirlwind of emotion that couldn't be neutralized. As experienced parents in the rhythms of angry pre-teen outbursts, my husband and I recognized the time for rebuking and discipline had arrived.

As we'd done before, we removed our frustrated girl from the chaotic ambiance to a room where we could calmly discuss the issues at hand. Firmly laying out the appropriate measure of disciplinary actions and praying together over the situation, my husband and I were settled that things were diffused. However, the victorious feeling of relief was surprisingly short-lived.

THE MESSINESS OF DISRESPECT

Sadly, the day had finally come when our discipline was no longer considered a feared consequence. As soon as we concluded the discussion, our daughter immediately pleaded her case once more, showcasing her unaffected attitude. As the arguing continued, my jaw hit the floor in astonishment. Her disrespect for our disciplinary governance gave way to an evolving sense of justice. She fought tooth and nail against the perceived mistrial, convinced that the scales should be tipped in her favor, regardless of her complete disregard for parental authority. Through this encounter, I came to understand the flippant fight I often put up against the Lord, tossing aside my healthy fear of him to protest my sinfully skewed points of contention.

As we grow, we find ourselves entered into a phase where independence and authority meet head-on. The more knowledge and experience we gain, the more intellectual ammunition we stockpile to make arguments, shape opinions, and reason away the wisdom set forth through rightful boundaries and restrictions. Standing up for one's rights is a good thing—certainly a freedom we enjoy in America—but it can lead us to a point where we've become too smart for our own good, focusing more on proving a point instead of seeing the big picture. These grounds can be a perilous minefield, not only for the young adult coming in to her own, but also for the developing child of God.

Being sincere with our heart reflections means we must be willing to confess our half-hearted fear of the Lord. We can get so consumed by the battle of wills in our home that we catch a case of spiritual amnesia, causing us to forget God's grace and ultimate lordship. When we sense our personal kingdoms under attack, we're prone to replace our duly reverence of God with an unwise fight for dominion.

WASHING WITH THE WORD

Wrestling with God out of arrogant fearlessness is certainly something we see to varying degrees throughout Scripture, whether it's literally as with Jacob in Genesis 32 or figuratively via the constant rebellion and disobedience of Israel. Though the Word yields copious examples of the constant yet futile battle between man and God over wills, it makes extremely clear whose plans ultimately stand (Isaiah 46:10) and that pridefully butting heads with the Almighty is sheer insolence (Proverbs 16:5).

Certainly our Father is big enough to handle our objections and misguided accusations; the Lord bids us to come and reason with him (Isaiah 1:18) and even faithful Job gave free utterance to his complaints (Job 10:1). Even so, if we habitually balk at his lordship over every aspect of our lives, we have not yet learned to savor a fruit ripened by humble surrender. We must rely on the Word and the Spirit to erase this line etched in the sand.

Will you even put me in the wrong? Will you condemn me that you may be in the right? Have you an arm like God, and can you thunder with a voice like his? Job 40:8–9 ESV

Respect for the Lord comes from a spiritual understanding of who he really is, one of those attributes being *just* (Jeremiah 9:23–24). The Lord is just in the same way a good judge rightfully balances law, evidence, and consequence to issue fair verdict. In essence, when believers hold in high regard a respect of the Lord, it isn't necessarily a fear that results in cowering dread, but rather an appreciation and acceptance that the God of the Bible has the authority to rightfully judge all of mankind (Ecclesiastes 3:17). Furthermore, this respect also recognizes his holy justice as completely warranted; his righteous judgments are always perfectly legal and joyfully vindicating (Proverbs 21:15).

Just as our daughter's waning respect for our disciplinary actions was evidenced through her relentless arguing, we too question our heavenly Father's authority with tireless fights to prove our case. We contend that there is a faulty decision to overturn, and as a result grow void of reverential awe for the One handing down the circumstances. Believing ourselves to be divinely wronged, we assume the position which yields the gavel of righteousness (Job 40:2). Unfortunately, we attempt to seat ourselves on this side of the bench more than we realize, especially when we've given ourselves over to the false entitlement that karma[2] preaches instead of the true justice of the Lord endowed through Christ (Titus 3:7).

Perhaps we're upset because we've been "really good" in our church attendance, or we've been trying hard to live an honorable life and yet still face hardships and pain. Maybe possessions or loved ones have been taken away from us through seemingly unfair circumstances, causing us to call into question the goodness and love of the Lord. Whatever the case may be, while we think we must argue for our "fair share", it's actually the *last thing* we should be petitioning for. We don't fully realize what we're asking when calling God's fairness into question.

Replacing well-founded reverence with a fight for fairness is an ignorant exercise. It completely ignores the unjust human suffering of Christ's passion and death—the cross being the pinnacle of God's generous justice towards sinners (1 Peter 3:18). Jesus was crushed under God's holy wrath, which in all *fairness* belonged to us. This is an unfair treatment we can actually rejoice in, because by it we are adopted into God's family.

A hearty respect of the Lord maintains the idea that we really don't want what we deserve, which is to be cast away to hell, separated from God's goodness and love for all eternity (Matthew 25:46). We offer the Lord reverence because he has the rightful power to treat us fairly (which would lead to our eternal demise), and yet his merciful grace showers us with forgiveness and blessings we could never merit through cavalier persuasions.

The friendship of the Lord is for those who fear him, and he makes known to them his covenant. Psalm 25:14 ESV

It's a strange thing to think that respectful fear and genuine friendship can go hand-in-hand, but when we look at what

God offers us through the gospel, we see yet another intriguing paradox that turns earthly wisdom on its head. Jesus Christ—God in the flesh—told his disciples they were his *friends* (John 15:15) and those whom God has given to him for salvation will know his voice when he calls them by name (John 10:27).

Being a friend of the Lord Almighty is not like groveling to an earthly king in order to be spared condemnation. While it's true that God's holy judgment will destroy those who aren't kept in his refuge (Luke 12:4–5), it is also true that he is patient with sinners so they may not perish but come to repentance (2 Peter 3:9). At first glance, this supreme power suggests a "ruling by fear" method of allegiance, but this isn't true of our Lord because in Christ a covering is available that shields us from God's justice. He used great power for great love. It is the acknowledgment of this balance that produces heart-transforming reverence, submission, and obedience.

God's love so permeates the Trinity[3] that not only does he himself settle the debt to bring sinners back into the fold, but he credits our accounts with the righteousness of Christ, making us not only clean but holy in his sight. When we have seen the beauty of the gospel of Christ, our godly fear produces wondrous awe and a confidence that the Lord will always be on our side as Father and friend (Romans 8:31). Even when things aren't going our way, this friendship affirms our hearts that God is up to something good (Romans 8:28).

Only fear the Lord and serve him faithfully with
all your heart. For consider what great things he
has done for you. 1 Samuel 12:24 ESV

This verse in Samuel holds the key for how we are empowered to serve the Lord—by considering what great things he has done for us. The hope we have to combat contention with God's authority is not found in trying harder to submit, but rather in growing more in our faithfulness, which is a product of the Holy Spirit's fruit in our hearts (Galatians 5:22).

Growth in reverence isn't a development we're able to fuel through our own efforts by simply recognizing a need to correct our attitudes. Everything, from our salvation to our submission, is a work of God's Spirit in our lives. Jesus affirmed to Peter it was ultimately the Father who revealed Christ to be the Son of God, and not a wisdom he had gleaned on his own accord (Matthew 16:17). It is by the testimony of the Holy Spirit we're able to see, understand, and appreciate God for all he is and all he has done for us (Hebrews 10:15–18). When we are given insight into the works of love God employed to sustain his people throughout history, we gain a stronger trust in his plan and a boosted desire to obey his commands.

Spirit-empowered reverence fuels Spirit-empowered faithfulness, and vice versa. The more we grow in one area, the more we grow in the other. As we practice this faith in God's sovereignty, we simultaneously grow our awe of the Lord, knowing his ways are higher and better than ours (Isaiah 55:8–9). And when we stumble over doubts and question his intentions, he continues his faithfulness to us as promised, because it never depended on our ability to perform in the first place (2 Timothy 2:13).

The very moments we find ourselves arguing against God's will for us, or some situation he has allowed into our lives, are the very moments we forget to recollect the things he has done for us as a people of God, as well as individually. Have we not heard of him turning dead bones into living bodies

(Ezekiel 37:3–10)? Has he not sealed his promises by rolling away the stone of Christ's tomb (1 Peter 1:3)? These are things Scripture reveals to us as majestic assurances of God's justice, grace, and faithfulness. Learning to humble ourselves to the Lord's authority means we do so by faith, confident we aren't bowing down to a tyrant who rules by fear, but rather a Father who leads through love.

BATHING IN PRAYER

Lord, today I bring to remembrance all of the work you have done in my life. While it's hard to see your plans in the moment, I can see the pattern of your faithfulness leading me up to this very hour. You don't give me the foreknowledge to know what lies ahead, but you do assure me that my feet will not slip as I walk in your ways. Father, I admit that the daily struggle to be my own god is a direct rebellion against my relationship with you. Sometimes I am so blindsided by my pride that I forget you delight to give grace to the humble. I surrender this battle to your hands, knowing that you gave me all when I could give you nothing. Though I could never repay you for what you have done on my behalf, I offer up my thanksgiving and praise. Give me peace as I rest in your presence, for I know that in you, through you, and for you are all things. In the name of the Father, the Son, and the Holy Spirit, amen.

HANGING OUR HEARTS OUT TO DRY
STUDY REFLECTIONS

Read Psalm 25:14. Continue to reflect on what the Bible says about revering our Father by looking up and examining three Scripture verses that touch on "fear of the Lord." Write the verses you find in your journal for quick reference in the future. (Tip: use your Bible's concordance in the back to look up these keywords or search your web browser by typing "Bible verse fear of the Lord")

MEMORIZATION

Only fear the Lord and serve him faithfully with all your heart. For consider what great things he has done for you. 1 Samuel 12:24 ESV

PRAYER

Read Job 40:1–9. Reflect on something you are currently wrestling the Lord about. Are you fighting against obedience, or perhaps for fairness? Write a prayer to confess this issue, ask for forgiveness, and thank God for the grace and truth given through his Son. If you are unsure where you might be resisting the Lord's authority, pray to the Spirit and ask him to convict you of any rebellion you may be currently blinded to.

Nothing will have been wasted.

On the far side of every risk—even if it results in death—
the love of God triumphs. This is the faith that frees us
to risk for the cause of God. It is not heroism, or lust
for adventure, or courageous self-reliance, or efforts to
earn God's favor. It is childlike faith in the triumph of
God's love—that on the other side of all our risks, for
the sake of righteousness, God will still be holding us.[1]

John Piper

8

Childlike Faith

"She didn't win." the text message read.

My husband had just learned the news as he picked up our daughter from school. As I mentioned previously, she had been running for Vice President of the Student Council. She organized the campaign all by herself, right down to the handmade bookmarks she distributed as promotional collateral. Earlier that day, we were talking about her excitement about the election as she wondered over the chance of winning. Rather suddenly, however, her confidence slid toward the other end of the spectrum; she began to share a creeping hunch the other candidate had garnered more votes.

"I'm pretty sure she got way more votes than I did." she laughed nervously.

"Well, how do you know that?" I replied.

"I asked a lot of kids and they all said they wanted to vote for her because they were friends. But it's okay, because even if I don't win I am going to run for President next year."

Her effortless confidence had knocked me off my feet. I was so proud of her in that moment, recognizing she had tossed aside any potential for disappointment that might come later in the afternoon. She had moved beyond the hypothetical fear of being rejected and went straight for the jugular of perseverance.

Later that morning, I encountered a tidal wave of my own fears. I struggled with the idea of writing this book and in doing so, opening up my messy heart for the whole world to see. As with any craft, the artist runs the risk of having their heartfelt creative expression completely jilted by critics and casual observers. Certainly sharing the intimate workings of one's own flailing path of motherhood and walk with Christ invites the potential for judgment and mockery.

What if I am rejected as a writer? What if people think it's foolish? Will they accept me for what I am and what I am not? Will I be able to handle the fear of failure? What if this is all just a waste of time and I'm chasing a passion that's never to be?

As I dabbled around a rabbit hole of doubts, I remembered our daughter's attitude about running for Vice President. Not once during our conversation did she share any concerns comparable to the ones I was stumbling over in my head. She had put her name out there on campus, presented a speech to an audience of fidgeting students, and yet had no fear of losing. Whatever the outcome, she would continue to pursue her goal of even grander distinction in the next school year. She wouldn't think twice about her loss, but would commit to press on toward the prize of being voted President next time around.

I hadn't expected to learn a lesson in faith through the youthful oblivion of a nine-year-old girl that day, but the Spirit used her attitude to reveal my hopeless hypnosis from hypothetical unknowns. I had taken my eyes off concrete certainties—mainly, my identity in Christ. I was convinced that any failure to succeed as a writer would also mean failure to succeed in the mission God had given me.

When pursuing our gifts for God's glory, we cannot entertain the belief that our failures to succeed translate to a failure of God's plan. When our sovereign Father carves out a path before us, any failure we experience is part of his plan, not a deficiency of it (Proverbs 19:21). If we lay our hearts on the line to pursue calling and things don't work out the way we'd hoped, we shouldn't view it as a mistake. Every step with faith in Christ is a step in the right direction.

Setting our hearts' desire on God's will means we don't have to ever doubt about being out of it. Just as the Lord knows the very hairs on our head (Luke 12:7), he also knows the steps we will take and the places we're destined to go (Proverbs 16:9). He says that he works *all things* for our good, including heartbreaking defeats and tragedies (Genesis 50:20). Weary sisters, we must continue to lean into the heavenly prize God is calling us to, just as the apostle Paul modeled for us centuries ago:

> *"I don't mean to say that I have already achieved these things or that I have already reached perfection. But I press on to possess that perfection for which Christ Jesus first possessed me. No, dear brothers and sisters, I have not achieved it, but I focus on this one thing: Forgetting the past and looking forward to what lies ahead, I press on to reach the end of the*

> *race and receive the heavenly prize for which God,*
> *through Christ Jesus, is calling us."* Philippians
> 3:12–14 NLT

Forgetting the past and pressing on toward Christ—this is what we need to remember when feeling consumed by shortcomings and failures. Embracing this endeavor means we can be as bold as lions to pursue God's calling on our lives (Proverbs 28:1). Having childlike faith in the Father means we can dream bigger than our imaginations can fathom without the fear of rejection or ridicule.

We can be certain that every trip, slip, fall, and sprint is part of a far greater plan. We don't need to crave the approval of others when we've already received it in Christ (John 6:37). It isn't about clean houses and mother-of-the-year awards, but about God conforming us to the image of his Son and the sweet fruit that comes from such a transformation. This pursuit may be folly to the world, but it is precious to the Lord (Isaiah 43:4). Like children who long to make their parents proud with crayon drawings, so too we offer our scribbled works to a smiling Almighty—not because we must earn his affections, but instead as a result of them.

CLOSING THOUGHTS

There's one point to which we must cleave as we draw near to the end of this book:

The mother who has experienced God's saving grace is also guaranteed his transforming grace.

So vast is the expanse of God's grace, that I could barely touch it here in these pages. Even still, I could not stress this point any more strongly. Those who have been redeemed by the blood of the Lamb can know with certainty that God is dead-set on giving them a pure heart and restored spirit (Psalm 51:10). You may not feel like you're growing leaps and bounds in your walk with Jesus, but God knows the change he is making and will not stop until the day you meet him face to face.

The true believer could never do anything to fall away from God's grace. You didn't earn your salvation by trying to live a perfect life in a spotless home, so too you cannot lose it by squabbling with your stubborn children or sobbing on the cold bathroom floor. Even still, genuine appreciation for endless grace does not cause daughters of the King to rejoice in sinful fancies (Romans 6:1–2), but rather it burns a fire of adoration for the Lord—a Father who gave everything to mend our messy, broken hearts.

Reflecting upon God's word together has encouraged us to hold tightly the promises of renewal and change. He isn't some high-and-lofty deity we cannot appeal to out of desperation. He isn't a master puppeteer pulling strings on the biggest stage of all time, cursing in frustration as our threads get tangled together. The Lord is intricately involved in every second of our life, knowing when and where to push or pull in order to draw us closer to his embrace.

Our Father isn't combing over the earth for those who are flawless homemakers; rather his eyes search to and fro looking for hearts that desire relationship with him (2 Chronicles16:9). Those clinging to the cross are the ones who receive unwavering strength and showers of mercy in their time of crippling need. Mothers who humbly learn to surrender present pride for a future glory are beautiful in the sight of the Lord (2 Corinthians 4:17).

The aches and pains of motherhood are not without generous rewards. The toothless grins, the slobbery kisses, the squeals of excitement when we walk through the door: these are the precious gifts of a loving Father who gives us a foretaste of the joy we'll experience in heaven (James 1:17). But even in the most humdrum situations, we can still sense the fire of anxiety tempting us to feel out of control and helpless. In times of disarray, we must remember God is on the throne, in control, and taking us right where he wants us (Ephesians 1:11). The challenges he permits to come our way (including bedtime tantrums and pre-teen tongue lashings) are not designed to magnify the problems within the hearts of others, but rather the ones buried within our own.

No matter how many times we scrub dried bananas off the floors, we never seem to keep them looking pristine. We may purchase all of the cleaning products the world has to offer, but unless we spare no expense in employing a full-time crew to continuously disinfect all our dirt and stains, we're doomed to suffer a filthy existence. Christ came to change all of that, not for our homes, but certainly for our hearts. No longer must we work tirelessly to present ourselves without blemish or spot, for Jesus said his very words have bleached us white (John 15:3). Our Savior may not have come to help with the housework, but he did come to help carry our burdens (Matthew 11:28), committing to be with us all the way to the very end (Matthew 28:20).

We recognize that God has paved the road to salvation and Christ is the way to eternal life, but without the Holy Spirit's power and guidance, our hope remains hidden from view. The Spirit is our coach in the corner of the pit; his steadfast leadership steps down into the slop where we wrestle with our heart, showing us how to get a tighter hold. It is there in the mire he picks us up battered and bruised, offering a clean robe of righteousness to cover our wounds and a stream of living water to quench our thirst.

If there be one thing we must pay special attention to as we learn to walk in the Spirit, it is to spend time with him reading and hearing God's Word. It is there God speaks to our hearts, using his instruments of redemption to perform surgeries and healings no human doctor could ever accomplish.

Struggling to enjoy and crave the Scriptures is not a sign of ineptitude, but is certainly a reason to seek out the fellowship of other believers or church small groups who can encourage your journey through the Bible. God designed us for community, and through that community Christ's encouragements are made manifest. Do not overlook the critical importance of being connected to a local church—you need the prayer, support, and mentorship of mature followers of Christ to minister to you as you walk with the Lord.

God provides the road, Christ provides the car, and the Spirit provides the gas. Certainly we can expect bumps and potholes on this crazy trip we call motherhood, but it doesn't change the course God has planned. Sometimes we're stuck on the side of the road waiting for a storm to pass. Other times, we're cruising along the coast watching the waves break and the birds dance in the sky. No matter the circumstances, God plans to reveal his glory and provision to us. Through life's flat tires and fender-benders, God's sovereignty and grace will shine forth. We may not always understand everything that happens on the road before us, but we can trust we'll see his goodness along the way (Psalm 27:13).

Dear overwhelmed mom, take heart! We're not all that different, you and I. Our messy hearts are equally desperate for God's transforming grace. I don't have this "mom-thing" figured out, and I don't believe God means that to be our goal.

We can let go of the facade that our lives should be completely in order, because the secret to a beautiful life is not to work harder at it, but to rest in the work Jesus has done. At the end of the day, it's not the work of our hands that makes our lives beautiful, but the breath of God, who spoke them to be from the very beginning.

Listen to me, descendants of Jacob, all you who remain in Israel.
I have cared for you since you were born. Yes, I carried you before
you were born. I will be your God throughout your lifetime—
until your hair is white with age. I made you, and I will care for
you. I will carry you along and save you. Isaiah 46:3–4 NLT

Study Suggestions for Small Groups | Leader Guide

Clean Home, Messy Heart can be used for individual or group study. Should you wish to lead a small group through this material, here are suggestions for how to organize the study sessions, facilitate meaningful discussion, and encourage in-depth reflection from your study participants. For more in-depth guidance, resources, and materials for leading a group through this book, please visit www.faithfulsparrow.com/CHMHsmallgroup.

- **Meet weekly. Eight total chapters allow for an eight week study.** You may wish to double up the chapters, but first consider discussing the option with your group, as you do not want to rush through the Scripture study and reflection questions provided at the conclusion of each chapter.
- **Consider methods of communication.** There are many ways of maintaining communication with your

group during your eight-week journey. A few of my favorites are via Facebook groups and text messages. If you and your group members are comfortable with Facebook, establishing a private group specific to your study might be a worthwhile option. This will allow chances for the group to share encouragements, prayer requests, quotes, verses, articles, etc. Getting everyone's phone numbers and starting a group text chain is another option, and of course there is always email. Any of these methods play an important part in encouraging fellowship and providing opportunities for the group members to minister to each other throughout the week.

- **Essentials: *Clean Home, Messy Heart*, a journal, a Bible, a pen, and a meeting place.** These are all of the ingredients for the study, paired with a commitment from each member to be faithful in their participation. I recommend using the Clean Home, Messy Heart Reflection Journal for your small group study—visit faithfulsparrow.com/CHMHjournal to learn more.

- **Lay a foundation of group expectations and privacy requirements.** Establish a consistent meeting time and stick to it, starting and ending on-time in respect for members. Discuss the need for privacy and confidentiality, especially because the study will pry into each member's heart struggles, and the results can be messy. If a member feels that they cannot make a confidentiality commitment, or you sense it might become an issue for the group, speak to an elder or mentor about suggestions on how to handle the situation based on the individual circumstances. Safety first—don't begin a study if you suspect confidentiality will be a concern.

- **Send meeting reminders the day before.** It's a good idea to check in with the group, to remind them of the upcoming meeting, alert them to any possible changes in time/location, and also to include a teaser about the topic of discussion based on the current chapter's theme.

- **Begin each meeting with an opening prayer and recap of the previous week's discussion.** As the group leader, always settle the minds and hearts of participants by leading them in prayer and asking for the Lord to bless the time spent together in his Word. Then, summarize the previous week's theme and discussion to focus on what the group has been learning about their own hearts thus far.

- **Ask participants to be prepared to report on how the Spirit has worked in their heart since the last meeting.** After recapping the previous week's theme and Scripture highlights, ask the group how they have been able to apply some of the Scriptures or chapter themes to their own personal situations.

- **Scripture Memorization.** This can be intimidating for many people, but by the power of God's Spirit, we can do it! Since each chapter's reflection section includes a memory verse, make it fun by having the group rehearse the Scripture aloud all together, or by writing the verses on individual note cards, adding them to a basket, and drawing a random card to see if the Scripture is recalled correctly. If so, the winner gets a prize (my discipleship group prefers chocolate bars)!

- **Comb through the current chapter as a group, asking participants to share thoughts, comments,**

or areas that spoke to them. This gives everyone a chance to contribute to the conversation and to further share how God may be using the material to appeal directly to their hearts.

- **Read the Scriptures!** Don't bypass the importance of letting God's Word speak to the group. At minimum, have the group read aloud the three main Scriptures in the *Washing with the Word* section as you review the chapter. As the leader, use your discretion to also dive deeper into the Scripture references in parenthesis to further solidify points, promises and/or truths. Prepare ahead of time to review parts of the chapter that the Spirit may be leading you to expand upon for the sake of discussion. You cannot overuse God's Word—it's what you're training the group to rely upon for growth. In addition, though the full verses of the featured Scriptures are provided in the book, I strongly believe in the benefit of each participant opening up their own personal Bible for the group reading.

- **Review the study reflection questions together.** Have each participant share their responses to the study reflection question. Encourage the group to take time in this area for thoughtful consideration. Also ensure that no one in the group is having difficulty answering the questions, looking up verses, or any other hindrances that may signify an area where one-on-one attention is warranted. As leader, be willing to mentor, train, and disciple those who may need someone to help teach them how to move around in their Bible or to search for verse themes online. We want to remove any stumbling blocks in this area, as God's Word is an essential part of maturing in Christ.

- **Review the prayer prompt responses together.** Each chapter concludes with a prompt for the reader to review Scripture and write out a prayer in their journal. This is designed to get the individuals concentrated on their heart reflections, confessions, and petitions to the Lord, and thus can become a very personal expression of faith. Use careful discretion here, depending on the dynamics of the group you are leading. You may not find it appropriate that each member read their entire prayer entry, but perhaps offer the chance to allow each person to share an overview of what they wrote and what they may be struggling with.
- **Conclude the discussion by collecting prayer requests.** Use this time to offer the group a chance to share specific personal prayer requests that the members can be praying over throughout the week. Follow up on the previous week's requests to see if there are any praise reports to share or updates the group should know.
- **Close the meeting in prayer.**

You will notice there are no questions at the end of the last chapter, but don't fret! I have provided them here for you to send out in advance of the meeting. You can also direct members to this page in the book as a reference for what they should be reflecting on in their journals for week eight.

WEEK EIGHT QUESTIONS:

- Which specific chapters in this book did the Spirit use to convict you of problem areas in your heart? If more than one, share the top two that really struck a chord with you.

- What have you learned about seeing your own heart struggles through interactions with your children?
- Are you beginning to hear the Spirit speak to you more clearly during chaotic times in your life? If yes, share a recent example. If not, ask the group to pray over you for this area and speak with your group leader about potential recommendations for improvement. (Don't be shy about this, and don't pretend, either! Let the group share your burden by helping to diagnose what may be distracting you from sensing the Spirit's leading.)
- Do you feel more confident and assured in God's transforming grace after going through this study? Why or why not?
- Overall, which spiritual discipline did you grow in the most (prayer, memorization, Scripture study)? Which would you like to improve upon?
- Conclude by writing a prayer that reflects upon the things you've read in this book, including major areas of contention, your dependency on God's grace for heart change, and a gratitude for bringing these struggles to mind so they can be healed by Jesus Christ, the Great Physician.

Once the study has concluded, you might find you've forged a bond that doesn't want to quit! You can visit my website faithfulsparrow.com for book recommendations—many of which are suitable for small group study. Be sure to celebrate the conclusion of your study with treats, goodies, and the pleasant aroma of Christ working in all of the lives of the women who have journeyed together through the book.

Lastly, I would love to hear feedback from you and/or the group participants about their time spent in the study. Please consider directing the group to www.faithfulsparrow.com/CHMHfeedback to complete a very brief survey. I want to hear the successes, hiccups, suggestions, and praise reports! The time you and the group take to provide these insights help me to grow in my gifting as well as ensure the quality of future editions and new title releases. You can also submit simple feedback or comments at my website www.faithfulsparrow.com/contact.

Thank you so much for considering *Clean Home, Messy Heart* as your small group material. I pray the Lord uses this little book in mighty ways for you, your group, and for those whom you may recommend the book to. I can't wait to hear what the Lord does through your study time together!

Resources

I have made several resources available on my website that will be helpful to you during your time in this book. Here are the various links you can use to learn more about the following topics and available tools:

The Gospel: The News You Need
www.faithfulsparrow.com/the-gospel

Getting the Most from Your Bible Study Time
www.faithfulsparrow.com/biblestudytips

Clean Home, Messy Heart Small Group Kit
www.faithfulsparrow.com/CHMHSmallGroup

Clean Home, Messy Heart Podcast
www.faithfulsparrow.com/category/podcast/

Clean Home, Messy Heart Study Journal
www.faithfulsparrow.com/CHMHjournal

Notes

CHAPTER ONE

1   Gloria Furman, *Glimpses of Grace* (Wheaton, IL: Crossway, 2013) 71, 72.
2   To be justified by Christ means to be declared righteous in the sight of the Holy Father solely because of the perfect life and atoning death of Jesus—not because of any effort or work on our part. Justification is solely a work of grace and not merits (Ephesians 2:8–9).
3   Lyric excerpt from the song, "How Deep the Father's Love for Us".
4   Golgotha is the hill where Jesus was crucified. An Aramaic word meaning "place of the skull," also known as "Calvary" in Latin.

CHAPTER TWO

1   Elyse Fitzpatrick, *Good News for Weary Women: Escaping the Bondage of To-Do Lists, Steps, and Bad Advice* (Seattle, WA: Tyndale House Publishers, Inc. in association with Resurgence Publishing Inc., 2014) 172, 179.
2   Original translations define the word *sin* as *to miss the mark*, which can be understood as missing the standard of perfection that God has set through his Law, the Ten Commandments (see Exodus 20:1–17).
3   The sovereignty of the Lord refers to his ruling over everything, in heaven and earth, even down to the daily happenings in our lives.

Because he is sovereign, he is always in control of the circumstances we face and constantly involved in the minutiae.

4   Meditation on God's Word is a key fuel for the believer in Christ. It is accomplished through the reading, listening and thoughtful consideration of the Scripture. The Biblical view of meditation means mulling over a selected verse or passage to listen to what God has to reveal to you through it. For tips on Bible meditation visit www. faithfulsparrow.com/biblestudytips.

CHAPTER THREE

1   Kevin DeYoung, *Crazy Busy: A (Mercifully) Short Book about a (Really) Big Problem* (Wheaton, IL: Crossway, 2013), 60.

2   God's goodness is part of his essence, meaning he doesn't only do good things, but he is good completely separate from any action or deed. His inherent nature is good (Psalm 119:68).

3   God is completely righteous, which means his character is infallible, perfect, flawless and majestically holy (Psalm 92:15).

4   The work of Christ refers to his sacrificial act as our sinless substitute, making it possible for repentant sinners to be welcomed into the presence of the Lord. Through suffering the complete punishment and wrath of God, he is able to exchange man's unrighteousness for his perfection. By doing so, he makes those who are born again by the Spirit acceptable before a holy God. This work restores the earthly and eternal *access to* and *communion with* the Father.

5   Witnessing as a believer in Christ is what happens when those outside the church watch, listen and experience God's work and love in our life. It can be an indirect testimony that someone is watching unfold from afar or a direct testimony that we share with someone face-to-face; in both cases, the goal in witnessing is to proclaim our belief in Christ, boast in the salvation he provides, and to invite others to partake of God's eternal grace and mercy.

CHATPER FOUR

1 Tullian Tchividjian, *Surprised by Grace: God's Relentless Pursuit of Rebels* (Wheaton, IL: Crossway, 2010), 32, 33.

CHATPER FIVE

1 Carolyn Mahaney & Nicole Whitacre *True Beauty* (Wheaton, IL: Crossway, 2014) 42, 44.

2 Being co-heirs with Christ alludes to our having been adopted as a child by God and therefore promised access to all of the glory of the Father as well as to rule alongside Christ in eternity.

CHAPTER SIX

1 Dietrich Bonhoeffer, *Life Together: The Classic Exploration of Christian Community* (New York, NY: Harper & Row Publishers, Inc., 1954) 95, 94.

2 Being the hands and feet of Christ means to actively serve as a part of the body of Christ, which is the church. Through the works of our hands and feet, Christ is able to bless others and demonstrate his love in tangible, visible ways.

CHAPTER SEVEN

1 Charles H. Spurgeon *The Treasury of David* on Psalm 128 (The Spurgeon Archive, 2001, http://www.romans45.org/spurgeon/treasury/ps128.htm#expl accessed 2/11/2016).

2 Karma is the Buddhist belief that a person who has done well in their life will receive good and the person who commits bad acts will earn bad—in essence, you get what you deserve.

3 The members of the Holy Trinity are God the Father, Jesus the Son, and the Holy Spirit. These are not three separate members operating independently of each other. They each are equally God of the universe, but also equally unique in their relationship

to each other. The Trinity is also expressed as *the Godhead three-in-one*, meaning three persons yet still one God.

CHAPTER EIGHT

1   John Piper *Don't Waste Your Life (Group Study Edition)* (Wheaton, IL: Crossway Books, 2007) 95.

About the Author

Christine M. Chappell is a wife and mother of three children. Her manuscript debut *Clean Home, Messy Heart* was awarded top ten honors in the 2015 WestBow Press New Look Contest. Christine has served in various leadership positions at Covenant Grace Church (Winchester, CA) and is currently focused on ministry of the Word at the local church level, with a passion for teaching and helping women dive deeper into the gospel. A former business owner and marketing trainer, she now balances home life with raising children and growing in Christ. Christine has been nominated for several community awards, including 2010-2013 Temecula Valley Chamber Young Professional of the Year and 2015 Murrieta Chamber 40 Under Forty.

Connect with Christine at her blog faithfulsparrow.com for articles, resources, book reviews, and podcast episodes. Find her also at facebook.com/cleanhomemessyheart, Instagram @ christinemchappell, and on goodreads.com/christinemchappell.

Printed in the United States
By Bookmasters